Valentines
a Collector's Guide

1700s - 1950s

Identification & values

COLLECTOR BOOKS
A Division of Schroeder Publishing Co., Inc.

Barbara Johnson, Ph.D.

4/11 Sad 10/10 1(0)

Front cover:
Top row: Rose chromolithograph valentine fan, "A Gift of Love"; 1901; $100.00 – 300.00. Flat valentine, Art Nouveau style children with a pansy and petal border; 1908; $8.00 – 18.00. Middle row: Fold down valentine, dapper boy wearing a top hat, lovebirds; Germany; circa 1920s – 1930s; $10.00 – 15.00. Mechanical valentine, dancing couple, upper bodies of the girl and boy move; U.S.A.; 1941; $7.00 – 13.00. Ornate fold down valentine with heart, girl, cupids, flowers, and cutwork; Germany; 1915; $50.00 – 55.00. Bottom row: Mechanical valentine, google-eyed clown and goose, goose's neck grows and shrinks, feet move; Printed in Germany; circa 1928; $25.00 – 35.00.

Back cover:
Top row: Sailboat and sailor boy valentine with honeycomb tissue paper heart; circa 1936; $12.00 – 18.00. Mechanical valentine of three children, legs move; Germany; 1931; $15.00 – 20.00. Row 2: Silver paper lace valentine, poppy and gold embossed layers, 3-D effects; circa 1890s; $25.00 – 35.00. Honeycomb tissue paper valentine, google-eyed children and hearts; Printed in Germany; circa 1920s; $45.00 – 55.00. Row 3: Flat die-cut valentine with easel, cupid taking a photograph amidst hearts; Printed in Germany; circa 1900s; $35.00 – 45.00. Bottom row: Mechanical valentine, cartoon-style boy, tongue and eyes move; Germany; circa mid 1930s; $20.00 – 30.00.

Cover design by Terri Hunter
Book design by Beth Ray

COLLECTOR BOOKS
P.O. Box 3009
Paducah, Kentucky 42002-3009

www.collectorbooks.com

Copyright © 2011 Barbara Johnson

The current values in this book should be used only as a guide. They are not intended to set prices, which vary from one section of the country to another. Auction prices as well as dealer prices vary greatly and are affected by condition as well as demand. Neither the author nor the publisher assumes responsibility for any losses that might be incurred as a result of consulting this guide.

Contents

Dedication

This book is dedicated to my mother Diane, my sister Michelle, and Mike. My mother Diane was indispensable in the creation of this book. She was tireless in her efforts to assist in the photography of the valentines to make them look wonderful. She wholeheartedly helped me with the organization, research, and manuscript preparation. Without her this book could never have been possible. I would like to dedicate the book to my sister Michelle whose love of antiques and a tenacious will to hunt out the best valentines wherever they might be found helped me find some of the choicest cards in the book. She devoted so much of her talents and time to helping me seek out some wonderful valentines. I would also like to dedicate this work to Mike who searched high and low with me on many search and discover missions to paper shows, antique stores, and flea markets to help me find some of the remarkable valentines depicted inside.

Introduction

Antique and vintage valentines are perhaps one of the most colorful and charming of paper collectibles. They are delightful marvels of design and true works of art. Their survival over the past two centuries despite their precious nature is a testament to everyone's fascination with them decade after decade. This book is intended to give the collector the most comprehensive means to date and value their cards. Valentine collectors oftentimes lack written records associated with the items they collect. Both World War I and II no doubt resulted in the destruction of much history about valentine makers, printers, and designs. Lacking such information, collectors can only use the facts available to advance the study of valentines. This includes a visual analysis of the actual cards and their design trends. Owner dated cards, whether labeled by the original sender or receiver, remain the best and most historically accurate means of organizing collections and valuing individual valentines.

As an historian I wanted to create a book that was the most efficient and comprehensive guide to identify and date valentines. I made it as historically accurate as possible in terms of organizing key facts. Each chapter lists important information about valentines including publishers, printers, and other crucial means of identification. The most valuable resources include detailed lists of popular valentine subjects, types of cards, and design features found chapter by chapter. Each list consists of important and thoroughly researched facts at the fingertips of collectors who can now identify their valentines with ease and speed. Dating a card puts it in the proper historical context and time frame. Spread throughout the book there are owner dated cards for almost every year chronologically from the 1880s to the 1950s and sporadically for earlier decades. I placed cards that had similar designs around these owner or sender dated "anchor" valentines to create chronological timelines within each chapter. My dating is conservative but it is extensively researched and available in a visual format for collectors to understand. Dates are given in rough ranges when there was a possibility the design features were used over several years. Since cards were oftentimes not labeled with the maker, printer, or designer, there is little documentation on the card itself to go on. Valentine collecting does not have to be a field steeped in mystery because we have little information. We can instead base our knowledge on what we do know and can easily see.

Much has been written in earlier works about companies and cards with subjects drawn by well known artists. The field has always lacked a reference guide that could organize, identify, and value all the other cards everyone has that constitute the majority of their collections, those that were mass produced, plentiful but anonymously published. These valentines have values equal to the cards made by well known makers but can be neglected because collectors lacked a comprehensive resource on them. Now the collector has a guide that puts these cards in a proper organizational or identifying order. Within these pages readers will see illustrated cards that are made, printed, or published in Germany, England, Canada, or the United States. Almost all cards illustrated are by anonymous makers. With certain exceptions, some Victorian to early twentieth century antique valentines published by well known firms are illustrated.

As a fellow collector, I wrote this book to be a visual guide that would be organized and easy for collectors of all levels to date and identify their valentines. It is not geared to be a history of printing techniques or a guide to publishing companies. This work focuses on the interpretations of valentine art and artistry through the ages. Most collectors will find very few valentines were signed or dated due to social customs and propriety through the ages. Nevertheless, anonymously published valentines were mass produced and easy for all of us to find. Not wishing to neglect published cards, a comprehensive system of lists is available for many non-illustrated cards that were published by well known firms. I incorporated lists of values for non-illustrated cards published by companies throughout the periods, particularly after World War I, so that collectors seeking values on these cards can find their worth quickly. This proper balance makes the book a thoroughly comprehensive reference for all collectors.

Valentines were mass produced making it easy for collectors to find cards. Valentine collectors will agree the cards are beautiful and charming in nature. Whether collectors seek cards from particular decades or themed subjects, they are equally satisfied with the unique varieties valentines have to offer. Antique paper enthusiasts are enthralled with nineteenth century chromolithograph scraps and beautifully engineered German fold down cards. Others are captivated by Dresden gold or silver scraps and delicate lacework seen on Victorian cards. One seeking valentines of well known companies like Raphael Tuck, Prang, Howland, or Whitney will never be disappointed with their splendid offerings. Collectors of animals, military subjects, famous characters from cartoons or comics, or transportation themes will also find their hunt for valentines equally delightful. Postcard enthusiasts will admire valentines for their marvelous renditions of children, women, and cupids similar to the beautiful postcard artwork of the early twentieth century. While valentine collectors are diverse in taste and scope, they equally admire this unique form of greeting card with every increasing year.

Valentine collecting is unique in the diversity of types of cards that have come into creation. The collector today can find the earliest valentines that were handmade, hand inscribed, and hand painted. Early nineteenth century examples represent the best of British and American printing, embossing, and designing, and are quite rare. Throughout the nineteenth century, British and later the earliest American cards reflected the finest examples of paper lace, embossing, applied embellishments, and chromolithography. Elevated by their multiple layers, these dimensional works of art achieved their presentation from the invention of the Victorian paper spring. This accordion-shaped paper spring made Victorian valentines a diorama of all the best the eye could see in resplendent colors, sparkling gold and silver,

and richly colored chromolithography. Valentines of the early twentieth century featured printed designs rather than collage-type designs put together by hand. Magnificent examples of three-dimensional fold down cards made in Germany continue to delight and amaze collectors. Some of the most charming valentines of the late nineteenth and early twentieth centuries were paper fans or multiple cards strung together and hung with ribbons or string.

As people entered into the twentieth century, their modern sensibilities and tastes changed. Valentines of the early twentieth century continued to be flat or fold down but we then see the fashionable trend toward the most adorable and charming of all card types, the mechanical valentine. Mechanical valentines began in the nineteenth century as novelty cards but they are rare and few survive today. Those of the twentieth century, first German then later American versions, are novel and clever. Mechanical cards displayed moving arms, heads, legs, and even full bodies after the pulling of a tab or lever on the card. They were cleverly designed and never boring. Most German mechanicals had two or more places of movement as compared to American cards with only one area of movement.

Valentines continue to mirror the concerns and mindsets of those who gave and received them. Cards from the 1920s began to show the fact that school children rather than adults continued the custom of card exchanging. As popular culture and customs changed, so did the themes of valentines. Cards of the 1920s to the 1950s are more juvenile in subject and aimed at appealing to school age children. The 1920s valentines show children in flapper age clothes or Art Deco artistic designs. Collectors of 1930s cards see children's interests in exotic animals, the everyday life activities of the young, and Depression-era clothing and hairstyles as key valentine features and subjects. When collectors approach cards of the 1940s some are patriotic and show the spunk and fortitude of a nation at war. Valentines of the 1950s show wholesome, juvenile subjects as America was now in a period of prosperity and security.

Many collectors will seek out the top named artists, manufacturers, or printing firms. Victorian valentine collectors will seek early British names like Meek, Mullord, Wood, Windsor, Dobbs, and Tuck. Early American valentine collectors search for Whitney, Howland, and Prang to name a few. Those who collect twentieth century cards might look to acquire those by Whitney, Carrington, or later firms such as Hallmark, Gibson, or American Greetings. The valentine collector has many different avenues in which to approach the kinds of cards he or she seeks. Others hunt for the wildly funny, rude, and insulting vinegar valentines as a bold alter-

Introduction ....

native to collecting sweet and sentimental cards. Collectors of everything unusual look for valentine fans, hanging cards, and three-dimensional honeycomb tissue paper valentines for something different.

Those who wish to start collecting valentines might wonder where to begin. Advanced collectors might want some ideas about where to look for more cards. Buying valentines has become quite easy today in the age of the computer. Internet auction sites, online antique dealers, and antique malls are wonderful places to find more treasures year round. Dealers of antique and vintage greeting cards or ephemera have a bevy of constantly replenished varieties. The older valentines are getting harder to find but are still out there. Collectors of Victorian valentines will find a treasure trove of beauties both here and abroad for sale in shops and on the internet. Some antique shops still have valentines tucked away amidst boxes of paper collectibles and postcards. Collectors might enjoy searching at ephemera and postcard shows for valentines.

Valentine card preservation is important for all collectors. Keep all valentines and any paper antiques free from dust and dirt. Keep them out of direct sunlight as the sun might fade them. If they are damaged, seek out someone who is a professional expert at paper conservation as an amateur repair of a card might damage it and will diminish value. All paper antiques including valentines must be kept in folders, albums, or boxes that are archival safe. If they are not, the acids from some plastics and papers can damage paper items forever. Make sure that these fragile items are supported so that they do not bend or tear. Try to save all pieces of broken valentines in case you wish to someday take it to a professional conservator to restore.

My values in U.S. dollars are given in ranges interpreted as fair market value for cards not entirely in mint condition to mint condition. As time progresses, collectors will find fewer mint examples of valentines, especially the older or more ornate ones. Prices were assigned a conservative range of high to low based on an exhaustive survey of hundreds of internet auction sales on popular websites during 2008 – 2009 and internet antique sellers and dealers at paper shows during these years. A word about condition is needed. I believe all antiques and collectibles have value whether they are in mint condition or not. I believe every piece however damaged still has value to someone and nothing should be ignored or discarded as it is a valuable part of our common history. Everyone's collection has cards that have damage. Condition of the cards you seek should be a matter best left up to the collector about what he or she wishes to pursue and purchase. I personally value my damaged cards just as I do my mint condition cards as all are almost irreplaceable pieces of art. As an historian I see them as vignettes of our cultural history. Both views need to be nurtured and expressed by collectors in this field.

Valentines are the most charming and endearing of all antique and vintage collectibles because they can tug at the owner's heart strings. Seeing hundreds of years of sentimental feelings and expressions of love is a window into the hopes and feelings our ancestors. Those who exchanged valentines did so according to the custom of their times. Whether by adult or child, the exchange of cards goes back centuries through time and spans many cultures. Valentines call to our minds nostalgic feelings of earlier times when we were children and exchanged cards at school. They are visually entertaining, witty, charming, beautiful to admire, and are delightfully poetic. Valentines are easy to find and are an affordable collectible for just about everyone. They have maintained a steady and consistent value in the marketplace. The cards remain one of the most beautiful of collectibles and antiques that never cease to amaze or dazzle.

Chapter 1
Eighteenth Century to 1839

Valentine's Day can be traced back to the ancient Roman festival of Lupercalia. This festival honored Pan and Juno, complete with a game where members of the opposite sex would draw lots and choose each other for the year. The Roman martyr St. Valentine, beheaded under the Emperor Claudius, has had his name attached to the holiday. For centuries people believed that birds chose their partners at this time of year. While the young sent anonymous cards and love tokens over the centuries, it is clear that the festivity of St. Valentine's Day still held.

Even after the English Reformation, people practiced the popular drawing of lots on the eve of St. Valentine's Day to chose a name from a vessel. This individual would be their "valentine" and possibly a future spouse. The English continued the superstitious belief that the first unmarried male meeting a young girl on the morning of St. Valentine's Day would be destined to be her husband.[1] Amidst centuries of social custom, people continued to honor St. Valentine's Day by exchanging valentines as tokens of love and affection.

Important Valentine Manufacturers, Publishers, and Printers

Eighteenth Century
Joseph Addenbrooke
Joseph Addenbrooke, an employee of Dobbs, was located at 101 Hatton Garden, London. He is reputed to have created and made paper lace as well as early valentines. Addenbrooke filed off the raised parts of embossed paper to innovatively achieve a paper lace effect.[2]

Alois Senefelder
Alois Senefelder invented lithography in 1798, a process using lithographic stones and different colored inks for color printing.[3]

1800 – 1809
H. Dobbs of London
Dobbs & Co. was established in London in 1803 and was one of the earliest manufacturers of fancy writing paper and stationery. Dobbs's patent is the earliest means of identifying the company. Dobbs valentines would later be labeled with Dobbs and Dobbs & Co. as identification marks up until the 1830s. The company was referred to as H. Dobbs & Co. in 1838.[4]

1820 – 1829
Engelmann Family
Engelmann family or Engelmann Graf Coindet & Company were German lithograph printers from 1829 to 1832.[5]

Mamelock & Adam
Mamelock was a German firm that manufactured scraps from the 1820s to the 1880s.[6]

John Windsor & Sons
John Windsor and Sons, of Vineyard Walk and later 2 Meredith Street of Clerkenwell, established himself as an English valentine maker and embosser from the 1820s to the 1850s.[7]

1830 – 1839
De La Rue & Company
Card makers, embossers, and fancy stationers, De La Rue of Cornish & Rock was located in London from 1831 to 1834. The company would be called James & Rudd De La Rue from 1834 to 1837. De La Rue and Company was established in 1835 at 20 Finsbury Place in London. From 1838 onwards the company was known as Thomas De La Rue & Co., Limited. It was in business until it was destroyed in World War II.[8]

Robert Elton of Elton & Company
Elton & Company was located at 18 Division Street in New York City. Elton is attributed to making valentines in 1833 but might have made valentines at an earlier date.[9]

Abraham Fisher
Fisher established his New York business in the early 1830s. He had a business in Philadelphia with Frederick Turner from 1835 to 1849. Fisher owned a book store at 90 Durson Street in 1836 and would be located at 52 Chatham Street from 1839 through 1845. He kept his book store at 74 Chatham Street in the 1850s.[10]

Joseph Mansell
John Mansell's firm dates from 1830 to 1902. Located at 35 Red Lion Square, London, Mansell made valentines in 1835 in his capacity as stationer, engraver, and printer.[11]

Turner & Fisher
Turner & Fisher was established in Philadelphia, Pennsylvania, from 1835 to 1849.[12]

Types of Valentines Illustrated

- Cut out valentines
- Paper lace valentines
- Pin pricked accent on the design valentines

Types of Valentines Not Illustrated

- Acrostic valentines, circa 1780s
- Copperplate printing, circa 1820s
- Cryptogram valentines
- Flower cage or cobweb valentines (German origin), a thread would lift up part of the design with a bee hive effect showing a picture or verse), circa 1796 to the1840s
- Hand-colored knotty shapes, circa 1760s
- Labyrinth designs, circa 1780s
- Lack of woodcuts and steel engravings before 1800 as they were too costly
- Love knot valentines in "quilt" patterns, circa 1780s[13]
- Love tokens, hand and heart cut work, circa 1800
- Love tokens with tape binding, inscribed, "binding their love" together
- Pen and ink valentines
- Pen work valentines
- Pennsylvania German or Fraktur style artwork
- Pin pricked design valentines, circa 1797
- Puzzle purse valentines, circa 1780s to the 1790s
- Puzzle valentines with verses needing deciphering
- Rebus valentines
- Theorem work or Poonah valentines, stencil cut watercolor flowers, circa 1835 to 1840
- Perforations in fixed patterns
- Water-colored valentines[14]

Design Features Illustrated

- Applied embellishments
- Dresden gold and silver scraps
- Embossing with hand painting
- Forget-me-not flowers
- Hand-painted ornament
- Handmade cuttings
- Paper lace
- Roses: meaning "much-charm"[15]

Design Features Not Illustrated

- Irises: meaning "message"[16]
- Lilacs: meaning (purple) "first emotions of love"[17]

Subjects Illustrated

- Birds
- Flowers
- Furniture
- Hearts
- Sailor themes and ships

Subjects Not Illustrated

- Angels
- Birds with hearts
- Cherubs
- Colors of red, green, blue, and yellow
- Fraktur or Pennsylvania-Dutch style painting
- Hearts
- Hymen's bower[18]
- Mating birds
- Patriotic themes in the early nineteenth century when Britain and France at were at war
- Red flowers and green leaves; circa 1835 – 1840
- Silhouettes
- Tulips: meaning in 1857 "a declaration of love"[19]
- Winged cupids[20]

Circular paper cut valentine with hearts and the initials, handmade; no publisher; printer markings: none; circa eighteenth century to early nineteenth century; no notice of copyright. $500.00.

Paper lace valentine with applied decoration and hand painting; publisher: Dobbs & Co.; printer markings: none; circa 1810s – 1830s; no notice of copyright. $250.00 – 500.00.

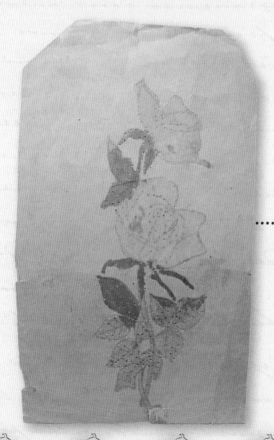

Pin pricked picture of hand-painted roses, handmade; no publisher; printer markings: none; circa nineteenth century; no notice of copyright. $55.00 – 85.00.

Paper lace with painted silk, applied silver Dresden scraps, flowers, and feathers; anonymous publisher; printer markings: none; circa 1810s – 1840s; no notice of copyright. $250.00 – 500.00.

Hidden message card, early mechanical art form, Empire style furniture, colored embossed paper; anonymous publisher; printer markings: none; circa 1800s – 1830s; no notice of copyright. $250.00 – 500.00.

Open doors reveal an affectionate message.

Hidden message card, early mechanical art form, colored embossed paper; anonymous publisher; printer markings: none; circa 1800s – 1830s; no notice of copyright. $250.00 – 500.00.

THE MEETING.

If angels in the realms of bliss,
The forms of earth descry,
With what delight they witness this
Sweet proof of friendship's tie.
Closer and closer let it prove,
The inseparable cord of love.

A flap opening the sail reveals a romantic message.

Chapter 2
1840 ~ 1849

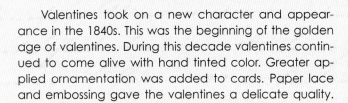

Valentines took on a new character and appearance in the 1840s. This was the beginning of the golden age of valentines. During this decade valentines continued to come alive with hand tinted color. Greater applied ornamentation was added to cards. Paper lace and embossing gave the valentines a delicate quality.

Hand-painted ornaments gave the valentines a unique vibrancy. The great majority of quality valentines were made in Britain but American valentine makers were capable of creating equally beautiful examples. Valentines of this decade are attractive to collectors for their sentimental nature and fine features.

Important Valentine Manufacturers, Publishers, and Printers

Dobbs, Bailey & Co.
Dobbs, Bailey & Co. of London were makers of lace paper valentines and some comic valentines during the 1840s.[21]

Elton & Company
Elton claimed to be the first publisher of American valentines in 1846. Robert Elton started as an engraver. He worked to make valentines at 18 Division Street in New York during the 1840s. This business was taken over by Thomas W. Strong, engraver, who worked at 153 Fulton Street and then remained subsequently at 98 Nassau Street.[22]

Abraham Fisher
Abraham Fisher of Boston, New York, and Philadelphia was an early maker of valentines working in New York from 1839 to 1845 at 52 Chatham Street then in the 1850s at 74 Chatham Street.[23]

Esther Howland
Esther Howland, born in 1828, enjoyed her first introduction to paper items from her father who worked as a stationer and bookseller in Worcester, Massachusetts, in 1849. She became a valentine maker in the 1840s.[24]

Keffer & Brett
John Keffer was recorded as an early lithographer in Philadelphia in 1839 and worked at 12 Bank Street in 1847. He was registered as J.L. Keffer in 1856.[25]

George Kershaw
George Kershaw and Son of London was a fancy stationer and seller of valentines and pictorial writing paper. He sold quarto valentines in the 1840s, smaller valentines in the 1850s, and fancy papers to others who made valentines.[26]

Jonathan King, Sr.
Jonathan King and his wife Clarissa were based out of London. A seller of valentines, Clarissa King was known for making fancy colored garlands and wreaths. She had the first notion of applying tinsel and feathers to valentines in 1846. The glittering tinsel on the cards was some years afterwards made by powdering broken glass. The firm continued through the death of Jonathan King, Sr. in 1869. The Kings used special materials on the valentine including rice paper, ribbon, silver lace paper, velvet, satin, swansdown, feathers, shells, pressed ferns, leaves, small artificial flowers, perfumes, French cambric roses, and pheasant feathers.[27]

McLoughlin Brothers
McLoughlin Brothers was located at 24 Belkman Street in New York from 1848 to 1950.[28]

Joseph Mansell
Mansell was based in London from the 1840s to the 1880s as a maker of embossed paper lace valentines, sachets, and greeting cards.[29]

George Meek & Son
George Meek of Crane Court, in Fleet Street, London, from 1840 to the 1890s, was a maker of embossed lace paper for valentines.[30]

D.W. Moody
Moody of New York was located at 140 Nassau Street in the 1840s. Moody was listed as David W. Moody, lithographer, in 1846, then as a draughtsman who was in business at 128 Fulton Street in 1849.[31]

David Mossman

Located in Islington, England, Mossman is known for valentines from the 1840s to the 1860s.[32]

Mullord Brothers

Mullord Brothers were paper lace makers for valentines in London from 1840 to the 1870s.[33]

Ernest Nister & Co.

Nister of London, New York, and Nuremberg, Germany, worked making moveable children's books then die-cut valentines from the 1840s to the 1890s.[34]

Other 1840s Valentine Makers

T.H. Burke of Newgate, England

Dean & Company (formerly Dean & Munday in the 1830s then Thos. Dean & Son) of Threadneedle Street, England[35]

Thomas W. Strong

This New York artist began work in 1842 at 153 Fulton Street and is later recorded in business at 98 Nassau Street in 1848. He was known for imported, domestic, sentimental, and comical valentines. Some beautiful examples were done stylistically in lace paper and gold.[36]

Turner & Fisher

The Philadelphia stationers Abraham Fisher and Frederick Turner worked together at 11 North Sixth Street up until 1849. Frederick Turner left to make valentines on his own as a publisher of lithographic valentines beginning in 1850.[37]

John Windsor

John Windsor is known as a card maker in 1840 in Vineyard Walk, Clerkenwell, England. He would be listed as a seller of prints and books in 1844. He becomes a card manufacturer located at 2 Meredith Street, Clerkenwell, in 1847.[38]

J.T. Wood & Company

Wood was located in London from 1842 to the 1870s and continued in business until 1905. He was a producer of embossed lace papers and comic valentines.[39]

Types of Valentines Illustrated

- Engraved printed valentines
- Hand-painted accents
- Poonah valentines
- Theorem valentines

Types of Valentines Not Illustrated

- "Bank of True Love" notes since 1847
- "Hymen's Temple" notes, since 1847
- Rebus valentines; circa 1841[40]

Design Features Illustrated

- Birdcage scraps
- Book scraps
- Cameo embossing
- Hand-colored pictures, 1840s to the 1860s
- Hand-painted features
- Lithographed pictures, 1840s to the 1860s
- Metal mirrors (intended for the receiver to see who was beautiful to the sender)

- Overall embossing
- Paper lace
- Personal name scraps
- Poonah or theorem valentines
- Watches scraps
- Wedding ring with inscription, late 1840s[41]

Design Features Not Illustrated

- American envelopes are hand stamped in 1845
- Artificial flower ornament introduced in 1845 by Mossman
- Embossed decorative letter paper from 1840 to 1842
- Envelopes with gummed flaps date after 1845
- Feathers
- French cambric roses
- Leaves
- Perfumes
- Pheasant feathers
- Pressed ferns
- Printed envelopes in Britain in 1840 due to the penny post
- Quarto size valentines with lace work seen in Britain

Chapter 2: 1840 – 1849

- Ribbons
- Rice paper
- Satin
- Sealing wax wafers used on envelopes prior to 1845
- Shells
- Silver lace paper
- Small artificial flowers
- Small central puzzle purses revealing sentiments
- Swansdown
- Velvet[42]

Subjects Illustrated

- Applied paper scraps with messages
- Children
- Couples
- Poonah or Theorem valentines, painted flowers

Subjects Not Illustrated

- "Unrequited Love" or "The Despondent Lover" sets of 14 aquatints of ladies and jilted lovers
- Birds mating, late 1840s
- Church with waiting coach, early 1840s
- Churches, early 1840s
- Cupids and hearts, early 1840s
- Glove motifs, 1849
- Lambs, late 1840s
- Lovers, early 1840s
- Men and women, early 1840s
- Pierced hearts, late 1840s
- Trees, early 1840s
- Urns, early 1840s
- Wedding ring pair interlocked, late 1840s[43]

Single heart valentines, hand-painted floral decorations, inscriptions: "Friendship's Wish," "Purity," and "I Request Farther Time My Sweet Roses You'll Spare"; anonymous publisher; printer markings: none; circa 1840s – 1850s; no notice of copyright. $75.00 – 120.00 each.

Hanging valentine, printed hearts with hand-painted decoration, inscriptions: "Friendship's Wish," "Purity," and "I Request Farther Time My Sweet Roses You'll Spare"; anonymous publisher; printer markings: none; circa 1840s – 1850s; no notice of copyright. $150.00 – 175.00.

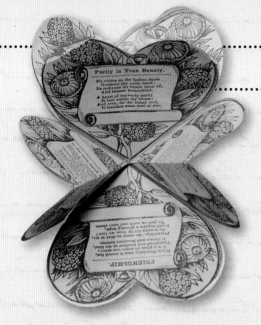

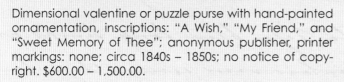

Inside view of dimensional valentine or puzzle purse below showing blue tinted paper with blue ink printed messages: "Purity is the True Beauty" and "Friendship."

Dimensional valentine or puzzle purse with hand-painted ornamentation, inscriptions: "A Wish," "My Friend," and "Sweet Memory of Thee"; anonymous publisher, printer markings: none; circa 1840s – 1850s; no notice of copyright. $600.00 – 1,500.00.

Inside view of dimensional valentine or puzzle purse above showing yellow-green tinted paper with blue ink printed messages: "A Golden Wish" and "Purity."

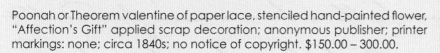

Poonah or Theorem valentine of paper lace, stenciled hand-painted flower, "Affection's Gift" applied scrap decoration; anonymous publisher; printer markings: none; circa 1840s; no notice of copyright. $150.00 – 300.00.

Hand-colored engraving with gold printed gilding and paper embossed
lace, applied verse scrap; anonymous publisher; printer markings: none;
circa 1845; no notice of copyright. $150.00 – 300.00.

Paper lace valentine with printed central decoration and applied
fold out paper with verses "Forget Thee, Oh, Never....," accompa-
nied by original stamped envelope (not shown); anonymous publisher; printer markings: none; circa 1848 – 1850s; no notice of copyright. $150.00 – 500.00.

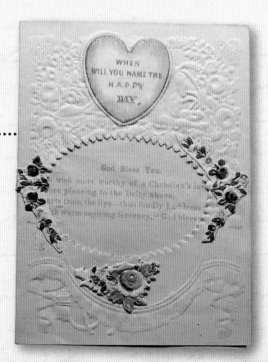

Embossed paper valentine with applied verse scrap "When Will You
Name The Happy Day" and "God Bless You," central interior verse;
anonymous publisher; printer markings: none; circa 1840s – 1850s; no
notice of copyright. $35.00 – 50.00.

Colored engraving; publisher: T.W. Strong; printer markings: T.W. Strong, N.Y.; circa 1840s; no notice of copyright. $150.00 – 300.00.

Printed engraving with hand coloring; anonymous publisher; printer markings: none; circa 1840s; no notice of copyright. $150.00 – 500.00.

Cameo embossed paper valentine, cameo embossed pastoral figure, scrolls, lover's knot, and flowers, "Constancy" scrap, applied glossy scrap personalizing the card "Louise," purple and green backing wafers, interior orange paper sheet, applied gold Dresden scrap, pasted interior verse; maker: Mansell; printer markings: embossed "Mansell" on card; circa 1840s – 1860s; no notice of copyright. $250.00 – 350.00.

Cameo embossed paper valentine in leaf pattern, applied paper wafers, wedding ring, and Dresden scraps, "Dearest I Am Truly Thine Own," pasted interior verse; maker: Mansell; printer markings: embossed "Mansell" on card; circa 1840s – 1850s; no notice of copyright. $150.00 – 300.00.

Cameo embossed paper valentine in scalloped pattern, central mirror (intended for the receiver to see who was beautiful to the sender), applied gold Dresden scraps and paper scraps, "Think of Me Still," pasted interior verse; publisher: none; printer markings: none; circa 1840s – 1850s; no notice of copyright. $150.00 – 300.00.

Cameo embossed paper valentine with cupid, bird, and floral garland design, paper wafer, silver birdcage Dresden scrap, "My Heart for Thine," pasted interior verse; publisher: none; printer markings: none; circa 1840s – 1850s; no notice of copyright. $200.00 – 350.00.

Cameo embossed paper valentine in pinpricked floral pattern, central mirror (intended for the receiver to see who was beautiful to the sender), applied gold Dresden scrap, paper wafer and paper scrap, "Thine Forever," pasted interior verse; publisher: none; printer markings: none; circa 1840s – 1850s; no notice of copyright. $150.00 – 300.00.

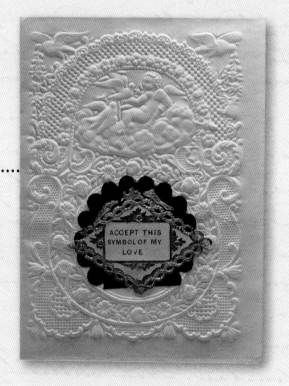

Cameo embossed paper valentine showing a cupid, birds, swags, and flowers, applied silver and white Dresden scrap, paper wafer, "Accept This Symbol of My Love," pasted interior verse; publisher: none; printer markings: none; circa 1840s – 1850s; no notice of copyright. $150.00 – 300.00.

Cameo embossed paper valentine in a scenic pattern showing a home, church, garden, trees, and figures, applied silver and gold Dresden scraps, paper wafer and paper scrap, "Dear Name the Day," pasted interior verse; publisher: none; printer markings: none; circa 1840s – 1850s; no notice of copyright. $150.00 – 300.00.

Cameo embossed paper valentine in pinpricked and scroll pattern with cupid holding a laurel amidst flowers, central mirror (intended for the receiver to see who was beautiful to the sender), applied gold Dresden scrap of a birdcage, "Be Mine," applied scrap of a woman, pasted interior verse; publisher: none; printer markings: none; circa 1840s – 1850s; no notice of copyright. $200.00 – 350.00.

Cameo embossed paper valentine in leaf pattern, applied gold and silver Dresden scrap, paper wafer and paper scrap, "Think of Me" and "Receive This Tribute of Esteem Now Due on This Recurring Day," pasted interior verse; maker: Mansell; printer markings: embossed "Mansell" on card; circa 1840s – 1850s; no notice of copyright. $150.00 – 300.00.

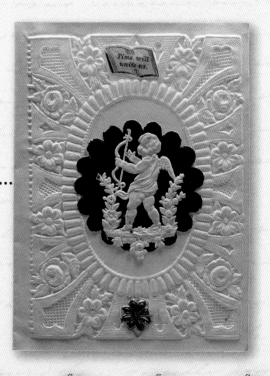

Cameo embossed paper valentine in floral pattern, applied cameo embossed scrap of cupid and bow, gold Dresden scrap, paper wafer, applied scrap, "Time Will Unite Us," pasted interior verse; publisher: none; printer markings: none; circa 1840s – 1850s; no notice of copyright. $150.00 – 350.00.

Cameo embossed paper valentine showing a bird, flowers, basket, and butterfly pattern, applied silver Dresden scrap, paper wafer, "I Could Love Thee Ever & Ever," pasted interior verse; maker: Windsor; printer markings: embossed "Windsor" on the card; circa 1840s – 1850s; no notice of copyright. $150.00 – 300.00.

Cameo embossed paper valentine in pinpricked floral pattern, central mirror (intended for the receiver to see who was beautiful to the sender), applied gold Dresden scrap, paper wafer and paper scrap, "Forget-me-not," pasted interior verse; publisher: none; printer markings: none; circa 1840s – 1850s; no notice of copyright. $150.00 – 300.00.

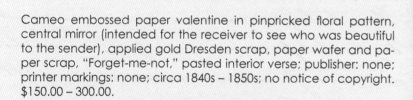

Cameo embossed paper valentine with an eighteenth century couple, cupids, a canopy with applied "Constancy" and "Sincerity" scraps, applied scraps and gold Dresden scraps, pasted interior verse; publisher: none; printer markings: none; circa 1840s – 1850s; no notice of copyright. $200.00 – 350.00.

Cameo embossed paper valentine with floral and scroll pattern, purple accents; publisher: none; printer markings: none; circa 1840s – 1850s; no notice of copyright. $150.00 – 300.00.

Cameo embossed paper valentine in pinprick and ivy pattern with pocket watch, applied gold Dresden scrap and paper scrap, "Thine Forever," pasted interior verse; maker: Mansell; printer markings: Mansell embossed; circa 1840s – 1850s; no notice of copyright. $200.00 – 350.00.

Cameo embossed paper valentine showing a forest, town, church in the background, figures, and garden scene, paper wafer, gold Dresden scrap, applied scrap of a book, "Dearest Love For Thee I Pine Come Be My Own Sweet Valentine," pasted interior verse; publisher: none; printer markings: none; circa 1840s – 1850s; no notice of copyright. $200.00 – 350.00.

Chapter 3
1850 ~ 1859

Valentines in the 1850s represent an even firmer design trend and manufacturing transition from cards personally crafted by hand to those mass produced by valentine makers. Diversified in their artistic features, British and American manufactured cards were more sophisticated, colorful, and elegant. British artistry was still superior to the infant American card industry.[44] American valentine makers continued to grow skillfully and artistically to progress and thrive along with the expertise of the British. *Harper's Weekly* reported only several hundred individuals were responsible for the industry that created the three million valentines sold in America in a given year. The Industrial Revolution brought important advances in technology as printing, embossing, and mass production improved progressively through the century. During the 1850s seventy-five percent of those who made valentines in America were women. Milliners were sought after because they made the best floral arrangements on valentines. Men ran the embossing presses while boys painted comic valentines.[45]

New York valentine shops were at the center of the trade in 1857. These businesses included P.J. Coyans, Fisher & Brothers, McLoughlin & Brothers, F.W. Strong, and J. Wrigley. An additional five or six valentine makers practiced their trade in New York, one in Worcester, Massachusetts, and two in New Hampshire. According to *Harper's Weekly* in 1857, valentines were popular through the Union. During the 1840s, traveling salesman combed the south and west with samples. During 1857, three million valentines sold. Half the valentines sold were comic and the other sentimental. People in 1857 paid three cents to three dollars for their valentines in the northern and New England states while those in the south and west averaged twenty-five cents to twenty dollars. The finest cards sold in larger cities for twenty to fifty dollars. Any card in the two dollar and up price range would be sold in a fancy box and be of Paris origin.[46]

Important Valentine Manufacturers, Publishers, and Printers

Dobbs, Kidd & Co.
Dobbs of London made lace paper valentines and some comical valentines during the 1850s – 1890s.[47]

Abraham Fisher
Fisher lived in his store in New York at Chatham Street to the year 1850. He moved to Philadelphia while keeping a book store at 74 Chatham St., New York, with branches in Boston and Baltimore. Fisher took on his brother working part time to become Fisher and Brother.[48]

Jonathan King, Sr.
Jonathan King, Sr. of London made large quarto sized valentines in the 1850s.[49]

Charles Magnus
Charles Magnus was a lithographer from 1850 to 1900, worked from 1854 to 1868 at 12 Franklin St., New York, and also maintained a business at 520 7th Avenue in Washington, DC during 1858 to 1865 +.[50]

Louis Prang
Louis Prang and Julius Meyer worked together from the 1850s to the 1860s. Their official company began in 1856. Prang was born in Breslau, Silesia, Prussia. He came to New York on April 5, 1850, and went to Boston where he published leather and wood engravings.[51]

Rock & Company of Walbrook
Rock & Company (W.H. Rock later Rock Bros. and Payne, London) were located in Walbrook, London, and printed valentines of quarto size in the early 1850s.[52]

Whitney Brothers
The three Whitney brothers Edward, Sumner, and George, of Worcester, Massachusetts, first made valentines independently. Sumner and Edward Whitney made valentines in 1858 then joined to form Whitney Brothers in 1859.[53]

John Windsor
John Windsor of England, already in business as a maker of enameled cards from the previous decade, made cards and fancy boxes at 23 Coppice Row, Clerkenwell in 1851. It is more than likely he created shadowbox valentines.[54]

Chapter 3: 1850 – 1859

Types of Valentines Illustrated

- Embellished envelopes
- Hand-painted lace cards
- Hand-tinted engravings
- Hanging valentines
- Lithographed valentines in color
- Small envelopes embellished with notes in the center of the card
- Theorem or Poonah valentines with stencil painted flowers
- Woodcut valentines

Types of Valentines Not Illustrated

- Bank notes, checks, and drafts from the "Bank of True Love" and "Hymen's Temple," 1847+
- Imitation "Love Office" telegrams [55]

Design Features Illustrated

- Artificial flowers
- Bright scraps
- Chromolithograph scraps
- Comical scraps
- English embossed paper
- English lace paper
- Engraved designs
- Engraved frame designs
- Gilding
- Gold embellishments
- Gold lace paper
- Hand-painted inscriptions
- Lace paper
- Leaves
- Paper flowers
- Paper lace
- Paper lace with flowers and leaves
- Printed flowers

- Printed verses
- Scrolls
- Small envelopes
- Small German scraps with love messages
- Verses of love or affection
- Virtuous sayings

Design Features Not Illustrated

- Crepe
- Hidden messages under flaps or petals
- Locks of hair sticking out of envelopes
- Lovers knots
- Medallions
- Mottoes
- One color printing
- Rice paper
- Satin centers
- Silver embellishments
- Silver lace paper [56]

Subjects Illustrated

- Children
- Couples
- Flowers
- Mushrooms or toadstools, insulting symbol meaning stinky, filthy, and proud [57]
- Roses meaning in 1857: beauty [58]
- Roses with leaves
- Scenes of outdoors, gardens, and lovers

Subjects Not Illustrated

- Classical columns
- Fountains
- Gondolas
- Medieval minstrals [59]

Embossed paper lace valentine with hand-applied floral and leaf decorations and painted captions; publisher: Dobbs, Kidd & Co., London; printer markings: embossed marking Dobbs, Kidd & Co. London; circa 1850s – 1860s; no notice of copyright. $100.00 – 175.00.

Printed valentine with hand-colored embellishments; anonymous publisher; printer markings: none; circa 1850s; no notice of copyright. $75.00 – 120.00.

Printed valentine with hand-colored embellishments; publisher: Charles Magnus; printer markings: CH. MAGNUS, No. 12 Frankfort Street, New York; circa 1850s; no notice of copyright. $75.00 – 120.00.

Chapter 3: 1850 – 1859

Comic valentine with embossed paper lace, chromolithograph scraps, applied paper decorations and painted caption; anonymous publisher; printer markings: none; circa 1850s – 1860s; no notice of copyright. $100.00 – 175.00.

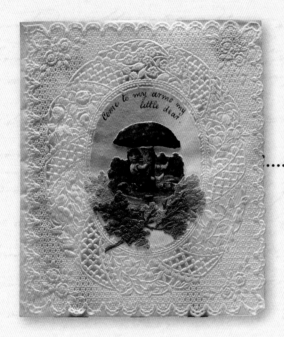

Embossed paper lace valentine with applied scraps, leaves, child, and mushroom or toadstool, verse; publisher: Dobbs, Kidd & Co., London; printer markings: embossed marking Dobbs, Kidd & Co. London; circa 1850s – 1860s; no notice of copyright. $100.00 – 175.00.

Close-up view of child, mushroom or toadstool, and foliage scraps.

Chromolithograph valentine with hand-applied gold Dresden scrolls and chromolithographs; anonymous publisher; printer markings: none; circa 1850s; no notice of copyright. $50.00 – 75.00.

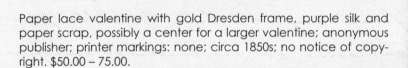

Paper lace valentine with gold Dresden frame, purple silk and paper scrap, possibly a center for a larger valentine; anonymous publisher; printer markings: none; circa 1850s; no notice of copyright. $50.00 – 75.00.

Hand-painted valentine with applied envelope decoration holding a printed message card; anonymous publisher; printer markings: none; circa 1850s; no notice of copyright. $100.00 – 175.00.

Chapter 3: 1850 ~ 1859

Close-up view of central envelope revealing a message card with printed verse.

Ornate printed envelope; anonymous publisher; printer markings: none; circa 1850s; no notice of copyright. $100.00 – 175.00.

Back view of printed envelope.

Chapter 4
1860 – 1869

The 1860s showed important design changes and features in valentines from the previous decade. Victorian valentines dating to the middle of the nineteenth century were engraved with lace paper borders and sometimes had heavy embossing. Senders sometimes wrote handwritten verses. Continuing to mirror earlier decades, 1860s valentines had hand-painted centers and cut paper lace borders.[60] The valentine industries in England and America continued to produce beautiful cards.

Valentines began to take on intricate artistry, color, and style due to their small yet ornate character. Romantic and delicate, these valentines were printed or hand assembled from English paper lace or German scraps. These examples grew more fanciful as time went on. The greatest of these examples had sachets for perfuming the card or open doors for hidden messages. Gold and silver embellishments made the colorful cards sparkle.

Important Valentine Manufacturers, Publishers, and Printers

Charles Goodall & Son
Goodall & Son was located in London from 1862 to 1885 where he made cards marked with his "Goodall" trademark, a heart intertwined with a ribbon.[61]

Thomas Goode
Thomas Goode, also known as Goode Bros. and Good Bros. (1913) Ltd., is known for making fake "love telegraph forms" during the 1860s.[62]

Esther Howland
Esther Howland of Worcester, Massachusetts, used embossed paper lace imported from such famous British makers as Mansell, Meek, Wood, Mullord, and Windsor. Her early cards are marked with a red "H." Esther Howland's unique idea regarding valentines was to use colored glazed paper wafers behind embossed details in order to accentuate the designs of the paper lace. She came up with the idea of abandoning the English assembly method of several lace paper motifs atop one another to use pieces that lift up and small centerpieces. She also added verse slips inside.[63]

Jonathan King, Sr. and Jr.
Jonathan King, Sr. and Jr., made smaller, octavo size valentines from 1860s onward. Jonathan King, Jr. and wife Emily Elizabeth continued making valentines after the death of Jonathan King, Sr. in 1869. They did business under the name E.E. King.[64]

Charles Magnus
Magnus of New York made Civil War era patriotic stationary as well as ballads, love songs, and serious and comic valentine sheets.[65]

Louis Prang
During 1860 Louis Prang dissolved his partnership with Julius Mayer. He was then known as L. Prang & Company in 1867 when he was located in Roxbury, Massachusetts. Here he reproduced chromolithographs and made Christmas cards. His cards entered the market at the same time as the cards of Marcus Ward and Raphael Tuck and Sons.[66]

Eugene Rimmel
Eugene Rimmel of the Strand in London made fanciful valentines in England and in his branches in New York and Paris. Rimmel worked in London from the 1860s through the 1890s. Rimmel's beautiful new valentines in the 1860s included perfumed sachets. These elaborate creations used perfumed cotton wool scented with lavender and violet. They would be placed in a padded and enclosed envelope that was highly decorated with embossed paper, silvered decoration, and scraps.[67]

Thomas Stevens
Stevens of Coventry, England, produced perfumed sachets that were hidden under a central motif of woven silk.[68]

Raphael Tuck
Tuck was a picture framer beginning in 1866 and a valentine exporter in 1871. He initially established himself in London but used German printers for his production.[69]

Marcus Ward & Co.
Marcus Ward & Company, a publisher of greeting cards, was located out of Belfast, London, and New York. He is known for using the artistic designs of Kate Greenaway and Walter Crane during the years 1866 – 1898. He started a lithographic firm in 1867 located in Belfast. Ward also went into the Christmas card business in London.[70]

Whitney Valentine Company, Whitney Manufacturing Company, and George C. Whitney

Edward Whitney managed Whitney Brothers after brother Sumner died in 1861. George joined in partnership with Edward in 1865 creating the Whitney Valentine Company. Edward left the partnership in 1869 to wholesale stationery and paper. George continued to make valentines as the Whitney Manufacturing Company. His business grew and he bought out his competitors. He purchased A.J. Fisher Company of New York and Berlin and Jones in 1869 among others. George C. Whitney of Worcester, Massachusetts, and New York City is recorded in business from 1866 to 1942 and is known as George C. Whitney Company, Whitney Brothers, and Whitney Manufacturing Company.[71]

Types of Valentines Illustrated

- Flat cards
- Fold down cards
- Fold out cards
- Sachets

Types of Valentines Not Illustrated

- Mechanical cards
- Vinegar valentines

Design Features Illustrated

- Applied embellishments
- Applied ribbons
- Applied silk trims
- Chromolithograph scraps
- Curves with point edges
- Dresden gold scraps
- Dresden silver scraps
- Embossed lace
- Glossy and thick paper
- Hand-painted features
- Lace embossing

- Lace paper backed by colored paper similar to wafer paper for design enhancement
- Lace scraps
- Mezzotints
- Paper lace in gold, silver, or colors
- Paper spring hinges used in later years
- Paper white lace
- Printed stationery
- Scraps at the center of the card with central frame
- Silk features
- Square edges

Design Features Not Illustrated

- Early Whitney valentines have bright lace paper
- Early Whitney valentines have colorful ornaments
- Early Whitney valentines have embossed envelopes from England
- Esther Howland cards used paper wafer discs
- Whitney cards have Mullord or Meek paper lace
- Whitney cards have a red "W" on the back
- Whitney cards used paper wafer discs[72]

Subjects Illustrated

- Angels
- Ballerinas
- Birds
- Cupids
- Flowers
- Romantic themes
- Roses meaning in 1857: beauty[73]
- Windows

Subjects Not Illustrated

- Military tents with flaps
- Soldiers and civilians[74]

Exact years in captions are original sender/receiver dates.

Paper lace valentine with gold paper lace, silk ribbon, and chromolithograph scraps; maker: Wood; printer markings: Wood embossed on card side; circa late 1850s – early 1860s; no notice of copyright. $50.00 – 75.00.

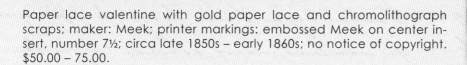

Paper lace valentine with gold paper lace and chromolithograph scraps; maker: Meek; printer markings: embossed Meek on center insert, number 7½; circa late 1850s – early 1860s; no notice of copyright. $50.00 – 75.00.

Paper lace valentine with gold paper lace and chromolithograph scraps; maker: Wood; printer markings: Wood embossed on side of card, number 7½; circa late 1850s – early 1860s; no notice of copyright. $50.00 – 75.00.

Green cameo embossed paper lace valentine with printed insert and gold Dresden wreath; anonymous publisher; printer markings: none; circa 1860s; no notice of copyright. $30.00 – 45.00.

1864

Paper lace valentine with silk insert, applied leaves, Dresden silver scraps; anonymous publisher; printer markings: none; 1864; no notice of copyright. $45.00 – 60.00.

1866

Paper lace valentine with insert and Dresden silver lace; anonymous publisher; printer markings: none; 1866; no notice of copyright. $35.00 – 50.00.

Paper lace valentine with Dresden gold paper lace and chromo-lithograph scraps; anonymous publisher; printer markings: none; circa 1860s; no notice of copyright. $35.00 – 50.00.

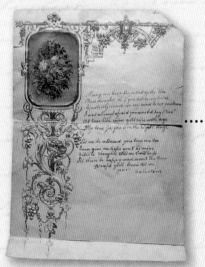

Embossed stationery with handwritten verse and printed scrap, gold embossing; anonymous publisher; printer markings: none; 1860s; no notice of copyright. $90.00 – 150.00.

1868

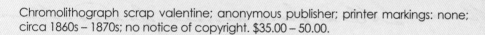

Paper lace valentine with drawing of young girl playing croquet; maker: Mullord; printer markings: Mullord embossed; 1868; no notice of copyright. $55.00 – 75.00.

Chromolithograph scrap valentine; anonymous publisher; printer markings: none; circa 1860s – 1870s; no notice of copyright. $35.00 – 50.00.

Paper lace valentine with Dresden and chromolithograph scraps; anonymous publisher; printer markings: none; 1868; no notice of copyright. $35.00 – 50.00.

Paper lace valentine, gold and cameo embossed lace and chromolithograph scraps; anonymous publisher; printer markings: none; circa 1860s; no notice of copyright. $50.00 – 75.00.

Green printed valentine with applied chromolithograph scraps; anonymous publisher; printer markings: none; 1860s; no notice of copyright. $35.00 – 65.00.

Paper lace valentine with gold paper lace, printed silk insert, and chromolithograph scraps; anonymous publisher; printer markings: none; circa 1860s – 1870s; no notice of copyright. $50.00 – 75.00.

Early paper lace mechanical valentine, hidden message card, silver paper lace, hand-painted message and embellishments; anonymous publisher; printer markings: none; circa 1860s; no notice of copyright. $65.00 – 85.00.

View of window open revealing a "With Love" message embellished with mica glitter, painted flowers, and leaves.

Valentine sachet card with hidden message beneath the chromolithograph scrap, "A Blessing"; maker: Wood; printer markings: Wood embossed on the edge; circa 1860s; no notice of copyright. $50.00 – 85.00.

Back view of sachet made from gold and white embossed paper lace showing a faux envelope design.

Valentine sachet card, silver and white embossed paper lace, silk insert message, "The Bridal Wreath"; anonymous publisher; printer markings: none; circa 1860s; no notice of copyright. $50.00 – 85.00.

Chapter 4: 1860 – 1869

Valentine sachet card with hidden message beneath the chromolithograph scrap, "A Wish"; anonymous publisher; printer markings: none; circa 1860s; no notice of copyright. $50.00 – 85.00.

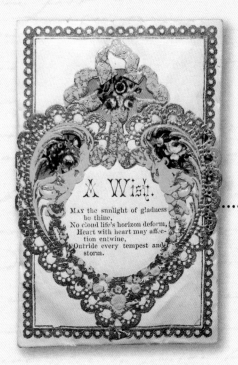

Valentine sachet with silk insert message, "A Wish"; anonymous publisher; printer markings: none; circa 1860s; no notice of copyright. $50.00 – 85.00.

Back view of sachet showing a printed scene of birds and flowers.

Gold paper lace valentine with insert; maker: Windsor, printer markings: Windsor embossing; circa 1860s; no notice of copyright. $35.00 – 50.00.

Chapter 5
1870 - 1879

The decade after the Civil War ushered in new changes for valentines. Valentines were being annually imported from England and Germany to America. These valentines bridged the design gap between a card using excessive lace to a completely chromolithographed card. What resulted was a valentine primarily white with small elements of color. This would transition into greater amounts of lace cutwork with color on the underside. Chromolithographs appeared as cards in their own right through the later 1870s. The tone of the 1870s valentine is ornate with a delicacy achieved through the decoration.

Important Valentine Manufacturers, Publishers, and Printers

Esther Howland

Howland continued making valentines and reorganized her business in the early 1870s to form the New England Valentine Company of 425 Worcester Street in Worcester, Massachusetts. She worked in connection with Edward Taft, the son of Jotham W. Taft. Howland's cards of this period would be embossed N.E.V.Co. and have a label with a red "H." Howland's cards have a small "H" red stamp on the upper or lower part of the back of the card. Her logos also include paper with a tiny white heart and a red "H" stamped upon the center. Other indications include a pasted label with an "H." Howland used English papers from makers like Mullord, Windsor, and Wood to create her valentines. Most markings were followed by numbers.[75]

McLoughlin Brothers

McLoughlin Brothers made valentines besides being prolific at producing books, games, lithographic items, and greeting cards from 1848 to 1950 in London. Markings on cards included a blue "H" on the upper right corner or a "Mc L" stamped on the card back. [76]

Charles Magnus

Charles Magnus was located in New York City at 12 Frankfort Street from 1854 to 1868, in Washington D.C. at 520 7th Street from 1858 to 1865, and is recorded back in New York City at 138 Canal Street from 1869 to 1871. During 1872 – 1873 Magnus worked at 550 Pearl Street in New York. [77]

Louis Prang & Company

Prang of Boston and Roxbury, Massachusetts, introduced his first Christmas card in America in 1875. Prang's themes included plain cards and silk fringed cards. Prang used images on his cards that had no symbolic association with the season including flowers, kittens, and scenes. Prang valentines dating from the 1870s are scarce. [78]

Rimmel

Rimmel of London made love telegraph valentine forms in 1871. [79]

Jotham W. Taft and son Edward Taft

Jotham Taft of Worcester, Massachusetts, made valentines in his own right and also created valentines for Howland and Berlin & Jones. Edward Taft was listed in Worcester as a valentine maker from 1877 to 1880. [80]

Raphael Tuck

Raphael Tuck of London made chromolithographs and black and white lithographs in the 1860s only to extend his business and make his first Christmas card in 1871. [81]

Marcus Ward

Marcus Ward of Belfast, London, and New York extended his business in the early 1870s to publish valentines. Ward's valentines featured old-fashioned children drawn by Kate Greenaway and Walter Crane. Crane and Greenaway were published in *The Quiver of Love*,[82] *a Collection of Valentines Ancient and Modern*, in 1876 showing four valentines from each of the two artists. These valentines were also published outside of the work with verses on the back as single or double cards. [83]

George C. Whitney

George C. Whitney of Worcester, Massachusetts, moved his business in 1874, and for the next eight years he made domestic valentines. At some point, Whitney bought out eight of ten competitors including Taft and Howland by 1888. Before 1876 he made only valentines, then he branched out to produce Christmas, New Years, and Easter cards, calendars, and booklets. Whitney continued to use his red "W" ink stamp on the back of his cards. [84]

Chapter 5: 1870 - 1879

Types of Valentines Illustrated

- Fold open cards

Design Features Illustrated

- Card divided into top and bottom horizontally with double themed designs
- Central ovals
- Chromolithograph scraps
- Design embossing
- Dresden gold or silver scraps in small amounts
- Envelope embossing
- Fringe
- Lace embossing (paper lace)
- Lace embellishments (fabric lace)
- Mesh fabric embellishments
- Paper embossing
- Paper spring hinges to raise designs
- Paper wafers
- Paper white lace
- Sawtooth edges
- Scalloped edges
- Scrap placed at center and in four corners
- Square shaped edges
- Thin paper quality

Design Features Not Illustrated

- Beads
- Boxed valentines

- Cambric flowers
- Dried berries
- Dyed moss
- Dyed seaweed
- Feathers
- Fir cones
- Heavier ornaments
- Sea shells
- Seeds
- Velvet flowers [85]

Subjects Illustrated

- Buds (rose) meaning in 1857: young girl [86]
- Couples
- Cupids
- Exotic themes
- Flowers
- Forget-me-not flowers meaning: true love [87]
- Ladies with satin or brocade dresses
- Old-fashioned couples
- Scenes of birds
- Scenes of gardens
- Scenes of homes
- Scraps are now centerpieces of the valentines
- Sweet animals
- Women

Exact years in captions are original sender/receiver dates.

1871

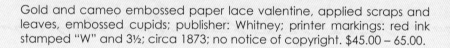

Paper lace valentine with 3-D effects; anonymous publisher; printer markings: none; circa 1871 – 1880s; no notice of copyright. $15.00 – 35.00.

1873

Gold and cameo embossed paper lace valentine, applied scraps and leaves, embossed cupids; publisher: Whitney; printer markings: red ink stamped "W" and 3½; circa 1873; no notice of copyright. $45.00 – 65.00.

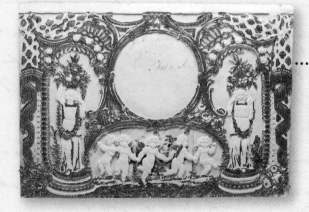

Gold and cameo embossed paper lace valentine, embossed cupids and classical figures, curtains (missing center scrap), interior applied scrap of verse; anonymous publisher; printer markings: blue ink stamped 2½; circa 1873; no notice of copyright. $40.00 – 60.00.

1874

Chromolithograph valentine; anonymous publisher; printer markings: none; circa 1874; no notice of copyright. $10.00 – 20.00.

1876

Chromolithograph valentine; attributed to Marcus Ward but unsigned; Walter Crane design unsigned; printer markings: none; 1876; no notice of copyright. $25.00 – 55.00.

Chromolithograph valentine; anonymous publisher; printer markings: none; circa late 1870s – early 1880s; no notice of copyright. $15.00 – 25.00.

Paper lace valentine with chromolithograph scraps; anonymous publisher; printer markings: none; circa 1870s; no notice of copyright. $35.00 – 50.00.

Woven silk message, fringe, silver paper lace, woven silk reminiscent of T. Stevens of Coventry; anonymous publisher; printer markings: none; circa 1860s – 1870s; no notice of copyright. $30.00 – 65.00.

Paper lace valentine with 3-D effects; anonymous publisher; printer markings: none; circa 1870s; no notice of copyright. $15.00 – 45.00.

Paper lace valentine; publisher: Whitney; printer markings: red ink stamped "W" for Whitney and 2½; circa late 1870s; no notice of copyright. $25.00 – 55.00.

Chromolithograph valentine; anonymous publisher; printer markings: none; circa 1870s – 1880s; no notice of copyright. $25.00 – 35.00.

Chromolithograph valentine; anonymous publisher; printer markings: none; circa 1870s – 1880s; no notice of copyright. $25.00 – 35.00.

Chromolithograph valentine; anonymous publisher; printer markings: none; circa 1870s – 1880s; no notice of copyright. $25.00 – 35.00.

Rare left-handed small paper lace valentine (opens to the right), chromolithograph scraps and paper wafer inserts; anonymous publisher; printer markings: none; circa 1860s – 1870s; no notice of copyright. $50.00 – 75.00.

Paper lace valentine with chromolithograph scraps and paper wafer inserts; paper maker: Meek Embossing; valentine maker: Taft with "10" mark; circa 1860s – 1870s; no notice of copyright. $35.00 – 50.00.

Paper lace valentine with 3-D effects; anonymous publisher; printer markings: red ink stamped "W" 1½ for Whitney; circa 1870s; no notice of copyright. $25.00 – 55.00.

Paper lace valentine with 3-D effects, fabric lace decoration; publisher: McLoughlin Brothers; printer markings: "Mc L." and "10"; circa 1870s; no notice of copyright. $55.00 – 85.00.

Paper lace valentine; anonymous publisher; printer markings: none; 1870s; no notice of copyright. $15.00 – 45.00.

Paper lace valentine with 3-D effects; publisher: New England Valentine Co., printer markings: embossed N.E.V. Co.& 15; circa 1870s; no notice of copyright. $25.00 – 55.00.

Paper lace valentine with 3-D effects, mesh fabric decoration; anonymous publisher; printer markings: none; circa 1870s; no notice of copyright. $15.00 – 45.00.

1879 – 1880

Paper lace valentine; anonymous publisher; printer markings: none; 1879; no notice of copyright. $15.00 – 45.00.

Rare left-handed (opens to the right) paper lace valentine; maker: Meek; publisher unknown; printer markings: lace paper made by Meek; circa 1870s; no notice of copyright. $45.00 – 65.00.

Paper lace valentine; made by Wood; printer markings: Wood paper lace embossed mark; circa 1879 – 1880; no notice of copyright. $25.00 – 55.00.

Paper lace valentine; made by Meek; printer markings: Meek embossed on the card's side; circa 1870s; no notice of copyright. $25.00 – 55.00.

Paper lace valentine; publisher: New England Valentine Company; printer markings: none; matching embossed envelope (not shown): N.E. Val. Co. 2; circa 1879 – 1880; no notice of copyright. $25.00 – 55.00.

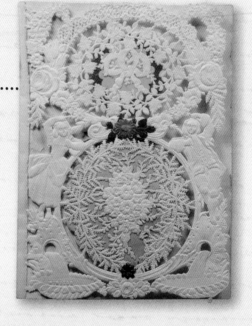

Paper lace valentine; made by Windsor; printer markings: Windsor embossed; 1879 – 1880; no notice of copyright. $25.00 – 55.00.

Embossed valentine; made by Windsor; printer markings: embossed Windsor; 1879 – 1880; no notice of copyright. $25.00 – 55.00.

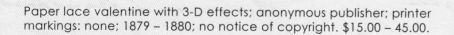

Paper lace valentine with 3-D effects; anonymous publisher; printer markings: none; 1879 – 1880; no notice of copyright. $15.00 – 45.00.

Rare left-handed paper lace valentine; anonymous publisher; printer markings: none; circa 1870s; no notice of copyright. $45.00 – 65.00.

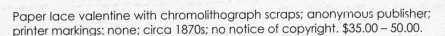

Paper lace valentine with 3-D effects; anonymous publisher; printer markings: none; 1879; no notice of copyright. $15.00 – 45.00.

Paper lace valentine with chromolithograph scraps; anonymous publisher; printer markings: none; circa 1870s; no notice of copyright. $35.00 – 50.00.

Paper lace valentine; lace paper maker: Meek; publisher: Whitney; printer markings: a sticker with "W" and 1½ indicating Whitney; circa 1870s; no notice of copyright. $25.00 – 55.00.

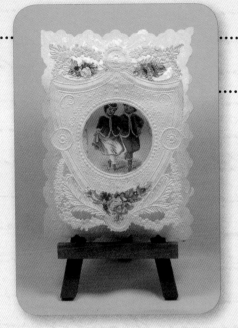

Paper lace valentine with 3-D effects; publisher: Whitney; printer markings: red stamped "W" and ½; circa 1870s; no notice of copyright. $25.00 – 55.00.

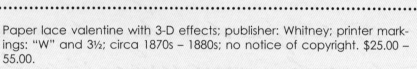

Paper lace valentine with 3-D effects; publisher: Whitney; printer markings: "W" and 3½; circa 1870s – 1880s; no notice of copyright. $25.00 – 55.00.

Paper lace valentine with 3-D effects; anonymous publisher; printer markings: none; circa late 1870s; no notice of copyright. $20.00 – 35.00.

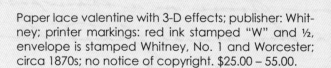

Paper lace valentine with 3-D effects; publisher: Whitney; printer markings: red ink stamped "W" and ½, envelope is stamped Whitney, No. 1 and Worcester; circa 1870s; no notice of copyright. $25.00 – 55.00.

Chapter 6
1880 - 1889

Valentines in the 1880s are distinctive and very characteristic of the well-known design motifs of the Victorian era. An abundance of paper lace with chromolithograph scraps provided a beautiful balance of the best of what both features offered to the design. Eastlake-inspired designs begin to appear. More color and bigger cards made valentines more noticeable and attractive to the eye. The paper springs under the lace layers gave the card greater dimension than ever before. Three-dimensional layers became more dramatic when accented with a variety of colors and designs.

During the 1880s Germany was still the best source for printing and lithography. The Germans were masters in the art of chromolithography which appeared on scraps on earlier greeting cards. Now chromolithography begins to dominate more of the design of the valentine. This process used different colored inks and a series of stones to create rich color printing that could be cheaply mass produced. Stunning effects and wonderful artistic achievements in valentine artistry resulted. Both American and English cards sold in their native lands had been printed in Germany. Even Raphael Tuck, a German immigrant and masterful artist, sent some of his designs to be printed in Germany to take advantage of their expertise and high quality. The tradition of having cards printed in Germany continued until World War I.[88]

Important Valentine Manufacturers, Publishers, and Printers

Esther Howland

Howland sold out to the George C. Whitney Company sometime between 1880 and 1881.[89]

Charles Magnus

Magnus was located at 1 Chambers Street in New York from 1884 to 1898.[90]

Louis Prang & Co.

Prang had made important strides in introducing his first Christmas card in 1875. During the 1880s he was known for his lithographic cards and silk fringed embellishments during the holidays.[91]

Raphael Tuck

Tuck was located at Coleman Street in 1881 as Raphael Tuck & Sons, exporters and chromolithographers. Raphael Tuck retired in 1882. His son Adolph took over. Tuck had a New York location from 1884 to 1944. Tuck had cards printed in England and Germany as well as distributing and selling cards in the United States. During the 1880s he published valentines and mechanical stand-up cards imported by other businesses from Germany.[92]

George C. Whitney

Whitney had bought eight out of ten major valentine producers before 1888 including Esther Howland's New England Valentine Company and Edward Taft's Taft, Grafton and Company. Whitney's cards were of embossed paper with a red "W." The final New England Valentine Company header is recorded in 1880. Whitney made valentines until 1876 then added Christmas, New Years Eve, Easter cards, calendars, and booklets. Whitney expanded from 1883 to 1910 only to suffer a fire that destroyed stock and machinery.[93]

Types of Valentines Illustrated

- Fold open cards
- Small cards
- Single sheet pages

Design Features Illustrated

- Chromolithograph scraps
- Chromolithograph cards
- Chromolithographs with touches of gold and silver
- Design embossing
- Dresden gold or silver scraps
- Eastlake styles
- Edges are pointed
- Edges are rounded corners
- Edges are sawtooth cuts and scallops together
- Forget-me-not flowers
- Four corner points with circles and then diamond points
- Fringe on chromolithograph cards[94]
- Gold printing on paper
- Lace cut outs
- Lace embossing
- Miniature scraps
- Multicolored embossed paper
- Paper spring hinges
- Paper wafers used less frequently
- Paper white lace
- Placement of chromolithograph scraps at the center of the valentine
- Placement of chromolithograph scraps at the center and four sides
- Placement of chromolithograph scraps at the center, top, and bottom
- White lace

Design Features Not Illustrated

- Embossed envelopes
- Paper quality: light to medium weight

Subjects Illustrated

- Angels
- Birds
- Children
- Cupids
- Dogs
- Flowers
- Ladies
- Old-fashioned adult couples
- Old-fashioned children
- Romantic scenes
- Scenes of churches
- Scenes of homes in winter
- Scenes of ships

Exact years in captions are original sender/receiver dates.

Chapter 6: 1880 – 1889

1880

Chromolithograph mechanical valentine; anonymous publisher; printer markings: none; February 14, 1880; no notice of copyright. $15.00 – 30.00.

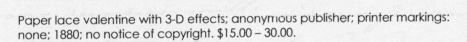

Paper lace valentine with 3-D effects; anonymous publisher; printer markings: none; 1880; no notice of copyright. $15.00 – 30.00.

Paper lace valentine with 3-D effects; anonymous publisher; printer markings: none; 1880; no notice of copyright. $15.00 – 30.00.

Paper lace valentine with 3-D effects; anonymous publisher; printer markings: none; 1880; no notice of copyright. $15.00 – 30.00.

Chapter 6: 1880 – 1889

Paper lace valentine with 3-D effects; anonymous publisher; printer markings: none; circa 1880; no notice of copyright. $15.00 – 30.00.

Embossed paper valentine with chromolithograph scrap; anonymous publisher; printer markings: none; 1880; no notice of copyright. $10.00 – 20.00.

Paper lace valentine with chromolithograph scraps; anonymous publisher; printer markings: none; 1880; no notice of copyright. $20.00 – 35.00.

Paper lace valentine with 3-D effects; anonymous publisher; printer markings: none; circa 1880s; no notice of copyright. $15.00 – 30.00.

1882

Paper lace valentine with 3-D effects; anonymous publisher; printer markings: none; 1882; no notice of copyright. $15.00 – 30.00.

1883

Chromolithograph flat valentine; publisher: Louis Prang & Company; printer markings: artist initials, L.C. and L. Prang & Co., Boston; copyright 1883. $15.00 – 30.00.

1884

Paper lace valentine with 3-D effects and insert; anonymous publisher; printer markings: none; 1884; no notice of copyright. $15.00 – 30.00.

Paper lace valentine with 3-D effects; anonymous publisher; printer markings: none; 1884; no notice of copyright. $15.00 – 30.00.

1885

Paper lace valentine with 3-D effects; anonymous publisher; printer markings: none; 1885; no notice of copyright. $20.00 – 35.00.

Chromolithograph valentine; anonymous publisher; printer markings: none; 1885; no notice of copyright. $15.00 – 30.00.

Paper lace valentine with 3-D effects; anonymous publisher; printer markings: none; 1885; no notice of copyright. $15.00 – 30.00.

Chromolithograph valentine; anonymous publisher; printer markings: none; 1885; no notice of copyright. $15.00 – 30.00.

1886

Chromolithograph valentine; anonymous publisher; printer markings: none; 1886; no notice of copyright. $15.00 – 25.00.

Paper lace valentine with 3-D effects; anonymous publisher; printer markings: none; 1886; no notice of copyright. $15.00 – 30.00.

1887

Paper lace valentine with 3-D effects on easel; anonymous publisher; printer markings: none; 1887; no notice of copyright. $20.00 – 30.00.

Paper lace valentine with 3-D effects, horizontal design; anonymous publisher; printer markings: none; circa 1887; no notice of copyright. $20.00 – 30.00.

Paper lace valentine with 3-D effects; anonymous publisher; printer markings: none; circa 1887; no notice of copyright. $20.00 – 30.00.

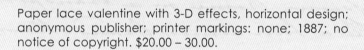

Paper lace valentine with 3-D effects, horizontal design; anonymous publisher; printer markings: none; 1887; no notice of copyright. $20.00 – 30.00.

Paper lace valentine with silk fringe on an easel, applied scraps, fluted paper; anonymous publisher; printer markings: none; circa 1887; no notice of copyright. $20.00 – 30.00.

Chromolithograph valentine; anonymous publisher; printer markings: none; 1887; no notice of copyright. $15.00 – 25.00.

Chapter 6: 1880 – 1889

Paper lace valentine with 3-D effects; anonymous publisher; printer markings: none; 1887; no notice of copyright. $15.00 – 25.00.

Chromolithograph valentine with fringed edging; anonymous publisher; printer markings: No. 234; circa 1887; no notice of copyright. $10.00 – 20.00.

Back view of fringe envelope style card showing a bird and nest.

Chromolithograph valentine with fringed edging; anonymous publisher; printer markings: none; circa 1887; no notice of copyright. $10.00 – 20.00.

Back view of fringed rose card.

1888

Paper lace valentine with 3-D effects; anonymous publisher; printer markings: none; circa 1888; no notice of copyright. $15.00 – 25.00.

Chromolithograph valentine; anonymous publisher; printer markings: none; 1888; no notice of copyright. $15.00 – 25.00.

Chromolithograph valentine; anonymous publisher; printer markings: none; 1888; no notice of copyright. $15.00 – 25.00.

Paper lace valentine with 3-D effects; anonymous publisher; printer markings: none; 1888; no notice of copyright. $15.00 – 25.00.

Chromolithograph valentine; anonymous publisher; printer markings: none; 1888; no notice of copyright. $15.00 – 25.00.

Paper lace valentine with 3-D effects; anonymous publisher; printer markings: none; 1888; no notice of copyright. $15.00 – 25.00.

Chromolithograph valentine; anonymous publisher; printer markings: none; 1888; no notice of copyright. $20.00 – 30.00.

Chromolithograph valentine; anonymous publisher; printer markings: none; 1888; no notice of copyright. $15.00 – 25.00.

Paper lace valentine with 3-D effects; publisher: Whitney; printer markings: "W" stamped in red ink with ½; circa 1888; no notice of copyright. $15.00 – 25.00.

Paper lace valentine with 3-D effects; anonymous publisher; printer markings: none; circa 1880s; no notice of copyright. $20.00 – 30.00.

Paper lace valentine with 3-D effects; anonymous publisher; printer markings: none; circa 1880s; no notice of copyright. $20.00 – 30.00.

Chromolithograph valentine; anonymous publisher; printer markings: none; circa 1880s; no notice of copyright. $15.00 – 25.00.

Paper lace valentine with 3-D effects; publisher: McLoughlin; printer markings: "Mc L" for McLoughlin and "5"; circa 1880s; no notice of copyright. $15.00 – 25.00.

Paper lace valentine with 3-D effects; anonymous publisher; printer markings: none; circa 1880s; no notice of copyright. $25.00 – 45.00.

Chromolithograph valentine; anonymous publisher; printer markings: none; circa 1880s; no notice of copyright. $15.00 – 25.00.

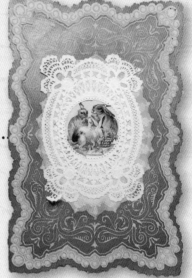

Chromolithograph valentine; anonymous publisher; printer markings: none; circa 1880s – 1900s; no notice of copyright. $10.00 – 20.00.

Paper lace valentine with 3-D effects; anonymous publisher; printer markings: none; circa 1880s – 1890s; no notice of copyright. $15.00 – 25.00.

Chromolithograph valentine; anonymous publisher; printer markings: none; circa 1880s – 1890s; no notice of copyright. $15.00 – 25.00.

Chromolithograph valentine; anonymous publisher; printer markings: none; circa 1880s; no notice of copyright. $10.00 – 20.00.

Chromolithograph valentine; anonymous publisher; printer markings: none; circa 1880s – 1890s; no notice of copyright. $5.00 – 10.00.

Chapter 6: 1880 – 1889

Chromolithograph valentine; anonymous publisher; printer markings: none; circa 1880s – 1890s; no notice of copyright. $5.00 – 10.00.

Chromolithograph valentine; anonymous publisher; printer markings: none; circa 1880s – 1890s; no notice of copyright. $5.00 – 10.00.

Chromolithograph valentine; anonymous publisher; printer markings: none; circa 1880s – 1890s; no notice of copyright. $5.00 – 10.00.

Chromolithograph valentine; anonymous publisher; printer markings: none; circa 1880s – 1890s; no notice of copyright. $15.00 – 25.00.

Paper lace valentine with 3-D effects; anonymous publisher; printer markings: none; circa 1880s; no notice of copyright. $15.00 – 25.00.

Chromolithograph valentine; anonymous publisher; printer markings: none; circa 1880s – 1890s; no notice of copyright. $15.00 – 25.00.

Chromolithograph valentine; anonymous publisher; printer markings: none; circa 1880s – 1890s; no notice of copyright. $25.00 – 35.00.

Chromolithograph scrap valentine; anonymous publisher; printer markings: none; circa 1870s – 1890s; no notice of copyright. $25.00 – 45.00.

Paper lace valentine with 3-D effects; anonymous publisher; printer markings: none; circa 1880s – 1890s; no notice of copyright. $25.00 – 35.00.

Chapter 7
1890 – 1899

Valentines in the Gay Nineties were some of the biggest and most elaborate of all time. Ornately ostentatious, they burst forth in an explosion of pastel colors accented with gold or silver lace layers and three-dimensional effects. The color palette included every shade of pastel.

These valentines made a breathtaking presentation due to their size and artistry. Cards in the decade used less paper lace than previous decades and more embossed layers. New shapes such as large hearts, squares, and crosses added interest and variety.

Types of Valentines Illustrated

- Fold open cards
- Larger valentines

Design Features Illustrated

- Applied embellishments
- Art Nouveau design elements
- Center of valentine has main design and ornament placement
- Center of valentine has oval with design inside
- Central frame has scraps in four corners
- Chromolithograph scraps
- Chromolithograph cards
- Color embossed backgrounds
- Design embossing
- Dresden gold or silver scraps
- Edges with sawtooth shape
- Edges with leafy rounded points
- Edges with pointed hearts
- Floral themes
- Glossy back papers
- Gold lace
- Ivory paper lace
- Lace embossing
- Lighter colored backgrounds
- Paper embossing
- Paper spring hinges
- Scrolls
- Silver and gold mixed in the background
- Silver lace
- Small central gold lace frames

- Small central silver lace frames
- Small central white with gold frames
- Small central white with silver frames
- Square cards
- Thin paper
- White embossed paper lace

Design Features Not Illustrated

- Four corners of the valentine have small scraps[95]
- Lace paper backed with colored paper to accent the details[96]

Subjects Illustrated

- Angels
- Bouquets
- Boys
- Butterflies
- Cupids
- Flowers
- Girls
- Ladies
- Old-fashioned couples
- Pansies meaning: thoughts[97]
- Romantic themes
- Roses meaning in 1857: beauty[98]
- Scenes of bridges
- Scenes of meadows
- Scenes of the ocean or water
- Scenes of outdoor homes
- Scenes of trees
- Scenes of windmills

Exact years in captions are original sender/receiver dates.

1890

Paper lace valentine with 3-D effects; anonymous publisher; printer markings: none; 1890; no notice of copyright. $10.00 – 20.00.

Chromolithograph valentine; anonymous publisher; printer markings: none; circa 1890s; no notice of copyright. $15.00 – 25.00.

1891

Paper lace valentine with 3-D effects; anonymous publisher; printer markings: none; 1891; no notice of copyright. $25.00 – 45.00.

Paper lace valentine with 3-D effects; anonymous publisher; printer markings: "F"; 1891; no notice of copyright. $15.00 – 25.00.

Chromolithograph valentine; anonymous publisher; printer markings: none; circa 1891; no notice of copyright. $15.00 – 25.00.

1892

Paper lace valentine with 3-D effects; anonymous publisher; printer markings: none; 1892; no notice of copyright. $20.00 – 35.00.

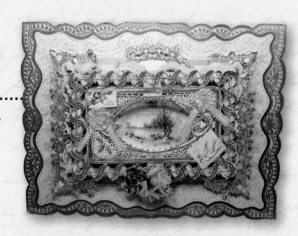

1893

Paper lace valentine with 3-D effects; anonymous publisher; printer markings: none; 1893; no notice of copyright. $25.00 – 45.00.

Paper lace valentine with 3-D effects; anonymous publisher; printer markings: none; 1893; no notice of copyright. $25.00 – 45.00.

1894

Paper lace valentine with 3-D effects; anonymous publisher; printer markings: none; 1894; no notice of copyright. $25.00 – 45.00.

1895

Paper lace valentine with 3-D effects; anonymous publisher; printer markings: none; 1895; no notice of copyright. $20.00 – 35.00.

Paper lace valentine with 3-D effects; anonymous publisher; printer markings: none; circa 1895; no notice of copyright. $20.00 – 35.00.

Paper lace valentine with 3-D effects; anonymous publisher; printer markings: none; circa 1890s; no notice of copyright. $20.00 – 35.00.

Paper lace valentine with 3-D effects; anonymous publisher; printer markings: none; circa 1890s; no notice of copyright. $20.00 – 35.00.

1896

Paper lace valentine with 3-D effects; anonymous publisher; printer markings: none; 1896; no notice of copyright. $15.00 – 25.00.

Paper lace valentine with 3-D effects; anonymous publisher; printer markings: none; 1896; no notice of copyright. $15.00 – 25.00.

Chromolithograph valentine; anonymous publisher; printer markings: none; circa 1890s; no notice of copyright. $15.00 – 25.00.

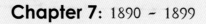

Chromolithograph valentine; anonymous publisher; printer markings: none; circa 1896; no notice of copyright. $15.00 – 25.00.

Paper lace valentine with 3-D effects; anonymous publisher; printer markings: none; circa 1895 – 1896; no notice of copyright. $15.00 – 25.00.

1897

Paper lace valentine with 3-D effects; anonymous publisher; printer markings: none; 1897; no notice of copyright; original envelope with 1897 postmark. $20.00 – 30.00.

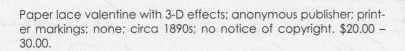

Paper lace valentine with 3-D effects; anonymous publisher; printer markings: none; circa 1890s; no notice of copyright. $20.00 – 30.00.

Chromolithograph valentine; unknown publisher; printer markings: "A"; circa 1890s; no notice of copyright. $15.00 – 25.00.

Chromolithograph valentine; unknown publisher; printer markings: "A"; circa 1890s; no notice of copyright. $15.00 – 25.00.

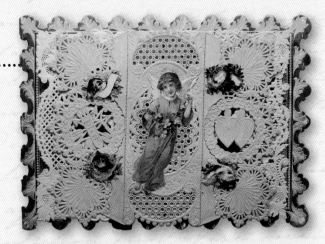

Paper lace valentine with 3-D effects; anonymous publisher; printer markings: none; circa 1890s; no notice of copyright. $20.00 – 35.00.

Paper lace valentine with 3-D effects; anonymous publisher; printer markings: none; 1897; no notice of copyright. $25.00 – 45.00.

Paper lace valentine with 3-D effects; anonymous publisher; printer markings: none; 1897; no notice of copyright. $25.00 – 45.00.

Paper lace valentine with 3-D effects; anonymous publisher; printer markings: none; circa 1890s; no notice of copyright. $25.00 – 45.00.

Chromolithograph valentine; anonymous publisher; printer markings: none; circa 1890s – 1900s; no notice of copyright. $15.00 – 25.00.

Paper lace valentine with 3-D effects; unknown publisher; printer markings: "G"; circa 1890s; no notice of copyright. $20.00 – 40.00.

71

1899

Paper lace valentine with 3-D effects; anonymous publisher; printer markings: none; circa 1899; no notice of copyright. $20.00 – 35.00.

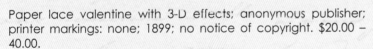

Paper lace valentine with 3-D effects; anonymous publisher; printer markings: none; circa 1899; no notice of copyright. $25.00 – 35.00.

Paper lace valentine with 3-D effects; anonymous publisher; printer markings: none; 1899; no notice of copyright. $20.00 – 40.00.

Paper lace valentine with 3-D effects; anonymous publisher; printer markings: none; circa 1890s; no notice of copyright. $20.00 – 35.00.

Paper lace valentine with 3-D effects; anonymous publisher; printer markings: none; circa 1890s; no notice of copyright. $20.00 – 35.00.

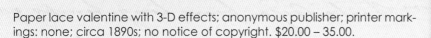

Paper lace valentine with 3-D effects; anonymous publisher; printer markings: none; circa 1890s; no notice of copyright. $20.00 – 35.00.

Paper lace valentine with 3-D effects; anonymous publisher; printer markings: none; circa 1890s; no notice of copyright. $20.00 – 35.00.

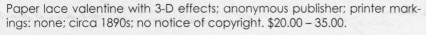

Paper lace valentine with 3-D effects; anonymous publisher; printer markings: none; circa 1890s; no notice of copyright. $20.00 – 35.00.

Paper lace valentine with 3-D effects; anonymous publisher; printer markings: none; circa 1890s; no notice of copyright. $25.00 – 35.00.

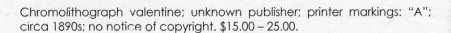

Paper lace valentine with 3-D effects; anonymous publisher; printer markings: none; circa 1890s; no notice of copyright. $20.00 – 35.00.

Chromolithograph valentine; unknown publisher; printer markings: "A"; circa 1890s; no notice of copyright. $15.00 – 25.00.

Chromolithograph valentine; anonymous publisher; printer markings: none; circa 1890s; no notice of copyright. $15.00 – 25.00.

Paper lace valentine with 3-D effects; anonymous publisher; printer markings: none; circa 1890s; no notice of copyright. $15.00 – 25.00.

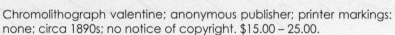

Chromolithograph valentine; anonymous publisher; printer markings: none; circa 1890s; no notice of copyright. $15.00 – 25.00.

Chromolithograph valentine; unknown publisher; printer markings: "A"; circa 1890s; no notice of copyright. $15.00 – 25.00.

Paper lace valentine with 3-D effects; anonymous publisher; printer markings: none; circa 1890s; no notice of copyright. $20.00 – 35.00.

Paper lace valentine with 3-D effects; anonymous publisher; printer markings: none; circa 1890s; no notice of copyright. $20.00 – 35.00.

Paper lace valentine with 3-D effects; anonymous publisher; printer markings: none; circa 1890s; no notice of copyright. $25.00 – 45.00.

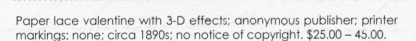

Paper lace valentine with 3-D effects; anonymous publisher; printer markings: none; circa 1890s; no notice of copyright. $25.00 – 45.00.

Paper lace valentine with 3-D effects; anonymous publisher; printer markings: none; circa 1890s; no notice of copyright. $20.00 – 30.00.

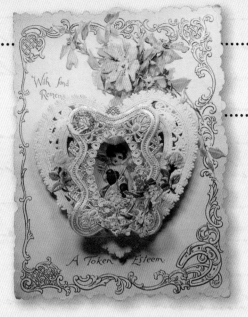

Paper lace valentine with 3-D effects; anonymous publisher; printer markings: none; circa 1890s – 1900s; no notice of copyright. $20.00 – 30.00.

Paper lace valentine with 3-D effects; anonymous publisher; printer markings: none; circa 1890s – 1900s; no notice of copyright. $20.00 – 30.00.

Paper lace valentine with 3-D effects; anonymous publisher; printer markings: none; circa 1890s; no notice of copyright. $20.00 – 30.00.

Paper lace valentine with 3-D effects; anonymous publisher; printer markings: none; circa 1890s – 1900s; no notice of copyright. $20.00 – 30.00.

Paper lace valentine with 3-D effects; anonymous publisher; printer markings: none; circa 1890s – 1900s; no notice of copyright. $20.00 – 30.00.

Chromolithograph valentine; anonymous publisher; printer markings: none; circa 1890s – 1900s; no notice of copyright. $10.00 – 15.00.

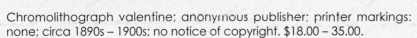

Chromolithograph valentine; anonymous publisher; printer markings: none; circa 1890s – 1900s; no notice of copyright. $18.00 – 35.00.

Chromolithograph valentine; anonymous publisher; printer markings: none; circa 1890s – 1900s; no notice of copyright. $10.00 – 15.00.

Chapter 7: 1890 – 1899

Chromolithograph valentine; anonymous publisher; printer markings: none; circa 1890s – 1900s; no notice of copyright. $6.00 – 10.00.

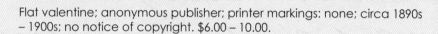

Flat valentine; anonymous publisher; printer markings: none; circa 1890s – 1900s; no notice of copyright. $6.00 – 10.00.

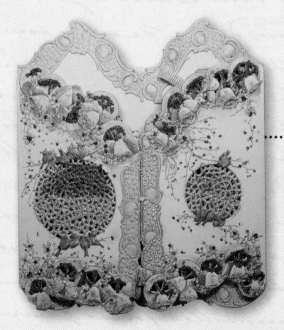

Fold open valentine with mica glitter and ribbon embellishments; anonymous publisher; printer markings: none; circa 1890s – 1900s; no notice of copyright. $15.00 – 25.00.

View of card opened to reveal the inner message and ribbon bow embellishment.

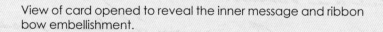

Sweet Valentine,
I send to You
Two bows of Ribbon, Pink and Blue;
If you often think, return the little bow of Pink;
If to me you'r always true,
Send me back the bow of Blue.
My heart is waiting for the time
To learn my thought.
My Valentine.

Chapter 8
1900 ~ 1909
Flat Cards

Valentines at the turn of the century represented new sensibilities and tastes. Cards were simplistic. Their elements of design were achieved more through printing than embellishments. One can see Art Nouveau themes emerge. Great profusions of flowers in bold colors decorate the cards. Many new companies would come into being during these years. Their early designs are somewhat scarce. Like English publishers, American makers seldom kept samples of the cards they first released for publication.[99] We can admire the cards we collect that survive as testaments to American greeting card ingenuity and taste.

Important Valentine Manufacturers, Publishers, and Printers

American Greetings
Jacob Saperstein arrived in America in 1905, moved to Cleveland, Ohio, and bought German-made post cards to sell to local shopkeepers. He eventually created American Greetings.[100]

The Buzza Rheem Company, later The Buzza Company, Minneapolis
Buzza began publishing greeting cards in 1909 with poster-like designs, a combination of print and hand coloring and heavy paper stock.[101]

A.M. Davis
Davis was a manager in 1906 of a Boston book store that distributed English and German cards. He began a line of his own in 1906.[102]

Gibson Art Company
Gibson Art Company began valentine production in the early twentieth century. Gibson had previously imported a large amount of German greeting cards. The company gradually learned American taste and the market needs, and began issuing its own designs in the early days of the company. Freelance artists were in New York and the design staff in Cincinnati.[103]

Fred Winslow Rust, Kansas City, Missouri, and later Boston, Massachusetts
Fred Rust began business in his bookshop in 1906. He would subsequently print his first Christmas card and further develop this business. He would be joined by his brother Donald in 1908 when they distributed cards throughout the United States.[104]

Paul F. Volland
Paul F. Volland of Chicago, Illinois, was a German native who began publishing in 1908 and a Christmas card line in 1909. He was known for exquisite offset printing, stock printing that harmonized with hand-coloring touches, and mottled and clouded design effects.[105]

Types of Valentines Illustrated

- Die-cut scrap cards
- Easel stand-up cards
- Flat cards
- Fold out cards
- Paper lace cards

Design Features Illustrated

- Black and white pictures as central designs around colored floral frames
- Embossed cards
- Gold accents
- Paisley style scrolls
- Paper lace
- Scalloped borders
- Scraps
- Subdued pastel tones

Subjects Illustrated

- Birds
- Boys
- Butterflies
- Carnations
- Children dressed in old-fashioned clothing
- Clover
- Clowns
- Cupids
- Daisies
- Floral garlands
- Floral swags
- Flowers
- Forget-me-not flowers meaning: true love[106]
- Girls
- Ladies
- Old-fashioned couples
- Pansies meaning: thoughts[107]
- Paper lace
- Pastel colors
- Poppies (red) meaning: consolation; (scarlet): fantastic extravagance[108]
- Wild roses
- Violets

Exact years in captions are original sender/receiver dates.

Die-cut valentine; anonymous publisher; printer markings: none; circa 1900s – 1910s; no notice of copyright. $12.00 – 20.00.

Fold open valentine; anonymous publisher; printer markings: none; circa 1900s – 1910s; no notice of copyright. $12.00 – 20.00.

Fold open valentine; anonymous publisher; printer markings: none; circa 1900s – 1910s; no notice of copyright. $12.00 – 20.00.

1900

Fold open valentine; anonymous publisher; printer markings: none; 1900; no notice of copyright. $6.00 – 18.00.

1902

Paper lace valentine with 3-D effects; anonymous publisher; printer markings: none; circa 1902; no notice of copyright. $20.00 – 40.00.

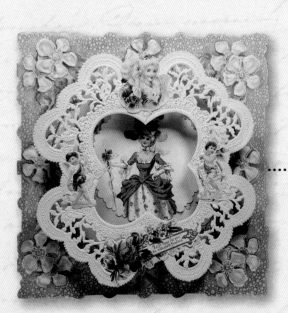

Flat valentine; anonymous publisher; printer markings: none; 1902; no notice of copyright. $20.00 – 40.00.

1903

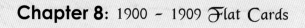

Fold open valentine; anonymous publisher; printer markings: none; 1903; no notice of copyright. $6.00 – 18.00.

Fold open valentine; anonymous publisher; printer markings: none; 1903; no notice of copyright. $6.00 – 18.00.

Flat valentine; anonymous publisher; printer markings: none; 1903; no notice of copyright. $6.00 – 18.00.

Fold open valentine; anonymous publisher; printer markings: none; 1903; no notice of copyright. $5.00 – 15.00.

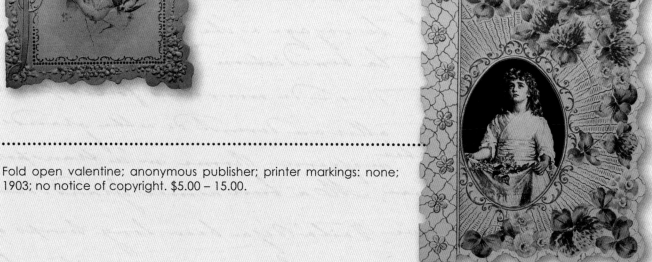

Chapter 8: 1900 – 1909 *Flat Cards*

Booklet valentine; anonymous publisher; printer markings: none; circa 1900s; no notice of copyright. $5.00 – 15.00.

Fold open valentine; anonymous publisher; printer markings: none; circa 1903; no notice of copyright. $5.00 – 15.00.

Flat valentines; unknown publisher; printer markings: "A"; on the top left, all others have no markings; circa 1903; no notice of copyright. $6.00 – 12.00 each.

Fold open valentine; anonymous publisher; printer markings: none; circa 1900s; no notice of copyright. $6.00 – 18.00.

Fold open valentine; anonymous publisher; printer markings: none; circa 1900s; no notice of copyright. $6.00 – 10.00.

Fold open valentine; anonymous publisher; printer markings: none; circa 1903; no notice of copyright. $5.00 – 15.00.

1904

Fold open valentine; anonymous publisher; printer markings: none; postmark on envelope 1904; no notice of copyright. $5.00 – 15.00.

Fold open valentine; anonymous publisher; printer markings: none; circa 1904; no notice of copyright. $5.00 – 15.00.

Flat valentine; anonymous publisher; printer markings: none; circa 1900s; no notice of copyright. $6.00 – 18.00.

Fold open valentine; anonymous publisher; printer markings: none; circa 1900s; no notice of copyright. $5.00 – 15.00.

Fold open valentine; anonymous publisher; printer markings: none; circa 1900s; no notice of copyright. $5.00 – 15.00.

Fold open valentine; anonymous publisher; printer markings: none; circa 1900s; no notice of copyright. $5.00 – 15.00.

1906

Fold open valentine; anonymous publisher; printer markings: none; 1906; no notice of copyright. $5.00 – 15.00.

Fold open valentine; anonymous publisher; printer markings: none; circa 1900s; no notice of copyright. $5.00 – 15.00.

Fold open valentine; anonymous publisher; printer markings: none; circa 1906; no notice of copyright. $10.00 – 20.00.

1907

Paper lace valentine with 3-D effects; anonymous publisher; printer markings: none; circa 1907; no notice of copyright. $10.00 – 20.00.

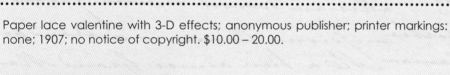

Paper lace valentine with 3-D effects; anonymous publisher; printer markings: none; 1907; no notice of copyright. $10.00 – 20.00.

Paper lace valentine with 3-D effects; anonymous publisher; printer markings: none; circa 1907; no notice of copyright. $10.00 – 20.00.

Fold open valentine; anonymous publisher; printer markings: none; circa 1900s – 1910s; no notice of copyright. $12.00 – 20.00.

Paper lace valentine with 3-D effects; anonymous publisher; printer markings: none; circa 1907 – 1910s; no notice of copyright. $25.00 – 45.00.

Paper lace valentine with 3-D effects; anonymous publisher; printer markings: none; circa 1907; no notice of copyright. $35.00 – 45.00.

Flat valentine; anonymous publisher; printer markings: none; circa 1900s; no notice of copyright. $8.00 – 18.00.

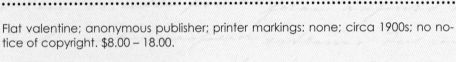

Flat valentine; anonymous publisher; printer markings: none; circa 1900s; no notice of copyright. $8.00 – 18.00.

Flat valentine; anonymous publisher; printer markings: none; circa 1900s; no notice of copyright. $8.00 – 18.00.

1908

Flat valentine; anonymous publisher; printer markings: none; 1908; no notice of copyright. $8.00 – 18.00.

Flat valentine; anonymous publisher; printer markings: none; 1908; no notice of copyright. $8.00 – 18.00.

Flat valentine; anonymous publisher; printer markings: none; circa 1900s; no notice of copyright. $8.00 – 18.00.

Flat valentine; anonymous publisher; printer markings: none; circa 1900s; no notice of copyright. $8.00 – 18.00.

Flat valentine; anonymous publisher; printer markings: none; circa 1900s; no notice of copyright. $8.00 – 18.00.

Flat valentine; anonymous publisher; printer markings: none; circa 1900s; no notice of copyright. $8.00 – 18.00.

Chapter 8: 1900 – 1909 Flat Cards

Valentine booklet with tassel cord; unknown publisher; printer markings: "E"; circa 1908; no notice of copyright. $6.00 – 12.00.

Flat valentine; anonymous publisher; printer markings: none; circa 1900s; no notice of copyright. $8.00 – 18.00.

Fold open valentine; unknown publisher; printer markings: "A"; circa 1900s; no notice of copyright. $8.00 – 18.00.

Fold open valentine; anonymous publisher; printer markings: none; circa 1900s; no notice of copyright. $6.00 – 15.00.

Flat valentine; unknown publisher; printer markings: "A"; circa 1900s; no notice of copyright. $8.00 – 18.00.

1909

Flat valentine; anonymous publisher; printer markings: none; 1909; no notice of copyright. $5.00 – 8.00.

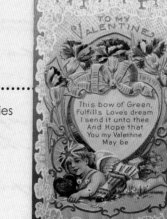

Postcard valentine; anonymous publisher; printer markings: Heart Valentine Series No. 2; postmarked February 13; 1909; no notice of copyright. $5.00 – 8.00.

Postcard valentine; anonymous publisher; printer markings: none; postmarked Feb 12; 1909; no notice of copyright. $5.00 – 8.00.

Flat die-cut valentine; publisher: Raphael Tuck; printer markings: Raphael Tuck trademark with easel; circa 1900s; no notice of copyright. $35.00 – 45.00.

Flat die-cut valentine; publisher: Raphael Tuck; printer markings: Raphael Tuck trademark with easel; 1900s; no notice of copyright. $35.00 – 45.00.

Die-cut valentine with easel; anonymous publisher; printer markings: none; circa 1909; no notice of copyright. $35.00 – 55.00.

Flat die-cut with easel; anonymous publisher; printer markings: none; circa 1900s; no notice of copyright. $35.00 – 45.00.

Flat die-cut valentine with easel; anonymous publisher; printer markings: Printed in Germany; circa 1900s; no notice of copyright. $35.00 – 45.00.

Fold open valentine; unknown publisher; printer markings: "A"; circa 1900s – 1910s; no notice of copyright. $8.00 – 15.00.

Fold open valentine; unknown publisher; printer markings: "C"; circa 1909; no notice of copyright. $8.00 – 18.00.

Flat valentine; anonymous publisher; printer markings: none; circa 1900s – 1910s; no notice of copyright. $10.00 – 20.00.

Fold open valentine; unknown publisher; printer markings: "C"; circa 1909; no notice of copyright. $8.00 – 18.00.

Flat valentine; unknown publisher; printer markings: "A"; circa 1900s – 1910s; no notice of copyright. $8.00 – 18.00.

Flat die-cut valentine; anonymous publisher; printer markings: none; circa 1900s – 1910s; no notice of copyright. $5.00 – 12.00.

Valentine booklet card, airbrushed accents; anonymous publisher; printer markings: none; circa 1900s – 1910s; no notice of copyright. $4.00 – 12.00.

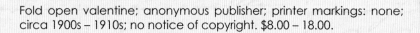

Fold open valentine; anonymous publisher; printer markings: none; circa 1900s – 1910s; no notice of copyright. $8.00 – 18.00.

Fold open valentine; anonymous publisher; printer markings: none; circa 1900s – 1910s; no notice of copyright. $8.00 – 18.00.

Fold open valentine; anonymous publisher; printer markings: none; circa 1900s – 1910s; no notice of copyright. $8.00 – 18.00.

Fold open valentine; anonymous publisher; printer markings: none; circa 1900s – 1910s; no notice of copyright. $8.00 – 18.00.

Flat valentine; anonymous publisher; printer markings: none; circa 1900s – 1910s; no notice of copyright. $8.00 – 18.00.

Flat die-cut valentine; anonymous publisher; printer markings: none; circa 1900s – 1910s; no notice of copyright. $15.00 – 25.00.

Fold open valentine; anonymous publisher; printer markings: none; circa 1900s – 1910s; no notice of copyright. $8.00 – 18.00.

Flat die-cut valentine; anonymous publisher; printer markings: Circle with "E" inside; circa 1900s – 1910s; no notice of copyright. $8.00 – 18.00.

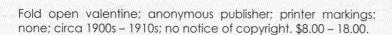

Fold open valentine; anonymous publisher; printer markings: none; circa 1900s – 1910s; no notice of copyright. $8.00 – 18.00.

Fold open valentine; anonymous publisher; printer markings: none; circa 1900s – 1910s; no notice of copyright. $8.00 – 18.00.

Chapter 9
1900 ~ 1909
Fold Down Cards

Fold down three-dimensional valentines were prolifically made in and imported from Germany from the 1890s through the 1930s. The perplexing issue of dating and identifying these cards stems from the fact that German printers and German manufacturers did not print their names on the cards. Not all of these cards necessarily stem from German businesses. A card printed in Germany could have been the product of an American valentine maker who sent designs to Germany to take advantage of German high quality printing. Other instances indicate cards of German origin were flooded into the American market by German valentine makers who monopolized the early industry. Germans faced difficulties or downside periods during wartime and from American import tariffs. The American greeting card industry was in an infant stage during those years. It faced stiff competition against German printing experience and quality craftsmanship. The Germans offered mass-produced, beautifully printed valentines at low prices. Adding to the mystery of these cards, most senders failed to sign or date them as it was thought to be bad luck.

Most fold down cards are marked "Germany," "Printed in Germany," "Printed in Saxony," or "Printed in Bavaria." Some American and other national firms who sent their valentines to be printed in Germany by German printers outside of wartime years, were still responsible for being the card's publisher and designer. German cards would not have been a popular purchase by Americans during times of war. No doubt war had a destructive effect on the card industry in terms of life and property losses. Although these stunning, dramatic, and quaint valentines will forever be a mystery due to the loss of historical records, current enthusiasts and future generations are, and will be, captivated by their beauty. Whether German made and exported for sale or designed in America and manufactured or printed in Germany for sale in America, the cards are lovely.

Anonymously Published Card
Markings Indicating Place of Manufacture or Printing

- "Germany"
- "Printed in Bavaria"
- "Printed in Germany"
- "Printed in Saxony"

Types of Valentines Illustrated

- Fold down cards with die-cuts
- Fold down cards with multiple layers

Design Features Illustrated

- German chromolithograph scrap

Subjects Illustrated

- Angels
- Boys in 1900s garments
- Cupids
- Flowers
- Gardens
- Girls in 1900s garments
- Period automobiles

Exact years in captions are original sender/receiver dates.

Fold down valentine; anonymous publisher; printer markings: none; circa 1900s; no notice of copyright. $12.00 – 20.00.

Fold down valentine (damaged tissue and top); anonymous publisher; printer markings: "Made in Germany"; circa 1900s; no notice of copyright. $10.00 – 14.00.

Fold down valentine, open view; anonymous publisher; printer markings: none; circa 1900s; no notice of copyright. $25.00 – 55.00.

View of central flap closed revealing cupids.

Fold down valentine; anonymous publisher; printer markings: "Germany"; circa 1900s – 1910s; no notice of copyright. $15.00 – 35.00.

Fold down valentine; anonymous publisher; printer markings: none; circa 1900s – 1910s; no notice of copyright. $15.00 – 35.00.

1902

Fold down valentine; anonymous publisher; printer markings: none; 1902; no notice of copyright. $8.00 – 15.00.

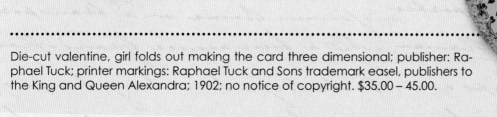

Die-cut valentine, girl folds out making the card three dimensional; publisher: Raphael Tuck; printer markings: Raphael Tuck and Sons trademark easel, publishers to the King and Queen Alexandra; 1902; no notice of copyright. $35.00 – 45.00.

1909

Fold down valentine; anonymous publisher; printer markings: none; 1909; no notice of copyright. $8.00 – 15.00.

Fold down valentine; publisher: Raphael Tuck; printer markings: Raphael Tuck & Sons, London, Paris & New York; circa 1900s – 1910s; no notice of copyright. $15.00 – 25.00.

Fold down valentine; anonymous publisher; printer markings: none; circa 1900s; no notice of copyright. $10.00 – 20.00.

Fold down valentine; anonymous publisher; printer markings: "Printed in Germany"; circa 1900s; no notice of copyright. $10.00 – 20.00.

Fold down valentine; anonymous publisher; printer markings: "Printed in Germany"; circa 1900s – 1910s; no notice of copyright. $8.00 – 15.00.

Fold down valentine; anonymous publisher; printer markings: "Printed in Germany"; circa 1900s; no notice of copyright. $15.00 – 25.00.

Fold down valentine; anonymous publisher; printer markings: "Printed in Germany"; circa 1900s; no notice of copyright. $15.00 – 25.00.

Fold out valentine; anonymous publisher; printer markings: none; circa 1900s; no notice of copyright. $10.00 – 20.00.

Fold down valentine; anonymous publisher; printer markings: none; circa 1900s; no notice of copyright. $25.00 – 55.00.

Fold down valentine; anonymous publisher; printer markings: none; circa 1900s – 1910s; no notice of copyright. $20.00 – 30.00.

Fold down valentine; anonymous publisher; printer markings: "Germany"; circa 1900s; no notice of copyright. $8.00 – 15.00.

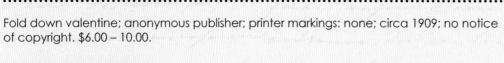

Fold down valentine; anonymous publisher; printer markings: none; circa 1909; no notice of copyright. $6.00 – 10.00.

Fold down valentine; anonymous publisher; printer markings: none; circa 1900s; no notice of copyright. $10.00 – 20.00.

Fold down valentine; anonymous publisher; printer markings: "Made in Germany"; circa 1900s – 1910s; no notice of copyright. $15.00 – 20.00.

Chapter 10
1910 - 1919
Flat Cards

Embodying the spirit and character of artistic movements of the period, valentines from the teens have their own unique and charming character. Collectors will find a greater number of anonymous cards in their collections. Before 1914 most of the valentines in the United States were imported from Europe. Whitney had competed with the imported products along with roughly 20 or more new American publishers at the start of World War I. A few additional American publishers made valentines. America no doubt had a distasteful feeling about doing business with German printers during World War I even though American cards were still not as aesthetically advanced as their German counterparts. Americans still embodied old-fashioned features on their valentines in the early teens including lace and embossing.[109]

During the war years, any foreign styles were removed from the market. A new type of American valentine would eventually emerge. More American in character and more friendly than sentimental, these new valentines were at the forefront of the industry. New "cute" valentines reflected America's unique social character. Later teens cards have new designs including children with cartoon-like features, old-fashioned attire, or chubby, adorable features. Once peace resumed, Americans kept their taste for the traditional and brought on a revival of lacey styles but the old English styles of verses were gone.[110] With less attention to romantic and loving thoughts on their cards, Americans turned increasingly to purchasing their own cards rather than imported versions. The new American valentines gave a friendly message and "up to the minute American humor, clean and wholesome, hand colored features." American cards distinctively used more red in their coloring.[111] Americans emerged from the Great War experienced at creating a new theme of greeting card that expressed their unique feelings and culture.

Important Valentine Manufacturers, Publishers, and Printers

Gibson Art Company
Gibson continued to produce greeting cards during this decade using free-lance New York artists and a staff of designers located in Cincinnati, Ohio.[112]

Rust Craft Publishers
Fred and Donald Rust continued with their greeting card business that would be known as Rust Craft in 1914.[113]

George C. Whitney
Tragedy struck the Whitney company in 1910 when a terrible fire destroyed the firm's plant and stock. Fortunately the valentines already produced had been distributed to the public. Whitney recouped his loss by purchasing his location at 67 Union Street in Worcester, Massachusetts. George Whitney would die in November of 1915.[114]

Types of Valentines Illustrated

- Chromolithograph die-cut valentines
- Die-cut fold out valentines
- Easel valentines
- Flat valentines
- Fold out valentines
- Lace embellished valentines

Design Features Illustrated

- Chromolithograph scraps
- Embossing
- Floral borders
- Paper lace
- Paper is thinner and shiny

Subjects Illustrated

- Art Nouveau floral themes
- Birds
- Cats
- Cartoon style characters
- Children
- Children's outdoor activities
- Cupids
- Flowers
- Girls
- Hearts
- Ladies in old-fashioned clothing
- Military themes
- Sailors
- Scenery
- Soldiers
- Transportation

Subjects Not Illustrated

- Buster Brown (1902 – 1920s)
- Campbell Soup Kids (1904+)
- Dolly Dingles (1913+)
- Kewpies (1909+)
- Sunbonnet Babies (1900+)

Published Cards Not Illustrated

"G" marking — possibly Gibson, Cincinnati, Ohio
Cards have a value of $4.00 – 18.00 each.
- 1910s – 1920s girl in wooden box horse cart, boy pulling cart, Gibson Art Company logo, an artist palette with "G" letter inside as trade mark, Printed in U.S.A.

International Art, Eagle on Globe logo
Cards have a value of $4.00 – 18.00 each.
- 1910s – 1920s nurse with medicine bottle

"Made in Germany"
Cards have a value of $6.00 – 20.00 each.
- 1917 era cat delivering valentine, pink door

Rose O'Neill
Cards have a value of $30.00 – 40.00 each.
- Heart-shaped card, two Kewpies, one sitting on green printed arm chair with a fan, the other kneeling down begging a proposal, notice of copyright Rose O'Neill and artist signed O'Neill

Raphael Tuck
Cards have a value of $15.00 – 40.00 each.
- 1910s – 1920s Dutch girl on golden polka dot wooden hobby horse, labeled Raphael Tuck & Sons, Ltd. London, Paris, Berlin, New York, Montreal, Printed in Saxony

Whitney
Cards have a value of $4.00 – 18.00 each.
- 1910s birds and roses, gold and stripes
- 1910s blue flowers, boy covering girl's eyes, small rectangular card
- 1910s boy fishing for hearts
- 1910s boy on roller skates, small heart
- 1910s boy with valentine at a door, small heart card
- 1910s child on wooden tricycle, small white and pink heart card
- 1910s couple with flowers, small red striped heart card
- 1910s girl and sailor boy, doll house, cut out card
- 1910s girl at a window, small heart-shaped card
- 1910s girl in left profile, roses, heart-shaped card
- 1910s girl in mop cap with butterflies, heart- shaped card
- 1910s girl in pink mop cap, black floral heart
- 1910s girl in pink sunbonnet, boy in overalls, blue flower border, heart with birds, farm scene in back
- 1910s girl sipping soda, lace overlay
- 1910s sailor boy, flowers, and butterflies
- 1910s small heart, girl with bonnet and heart package
- 1916 boy with axe, "No Trespassing," heart- shaped top, square shaped bottom
- 1910s – 1920s blue, purple, green, and yellow butterfly with heart insert, purple checkered and rose border
- 1910s – 1920s boy and girl profiles in gold hearts, pur-

ple background, blue, yellow, and green butterflies

- 1910s – 1920s boy at garden sundial, lace overlay, butterfly and Art Deco border, butterfly girl applied scraps
- 1910s – 1920s boy in blue suit, large farm hat, package, bouquet of roses, Art Deco border, lace overlay, applied scraps
- 1910s – 1920s boy in blue suit, small heart card
- 1910s – 1920s boy in red sweater, small heart card
- 1910s – 1920s boy showing left profile, heart-shaped top, and rectangular bottom
- 1910s – 1920s boy waiting at green door in wall, girl looking on from above
- 1910s – 1920s boy with baseball bat, dog, lace overlay, applied scraps
- 1910s – 1920s boy with pink flowers, small heart card
- 1910s – 1920s child eating ice cream, diamond lace overlay, daffodils and yellow flower borders, applied scraps
- 1910s – 1920s child in wooden go-cart
- 1910s – 1920s couple in old-fashioned dress, flower bouquet, small rectangular card
- 1910s – 1920s couple silhouette, black lace overlay, large rectangular card
- 1910s – 1920s couple under umbrella, lace overlay, airplane and heart applied scraps
- 1910s – 1920s cupid pushing girl on rope swing
- 1910s – 1920s cut out easel card, girl in yellow bonnet, full blue floral dress, rose print
- 1910s – 1920s double side fold open, girl and boy sitting, girl and boy pulling ribbon to untie hearts
- 1910s – 1920s farmer boy in black hat, small heart card
- 1910s – 1920s girl and boy by fence post both carrying pussy willow bunches
- 1910s – 1920s girl and boy ice skating, heart insert, border, wild roses
- 1910s – 1920s girl and boy on old tricycle, blue flowers, Art Deco border
- 1910s – 1920s girl at window with curtains, heart-shaped card, hanging birdcages
- 1910s – 1920s girl in blue dress knitting
- 1910s – 1920s girl in blue drop waist dress, cloche hat, standing on paving stones waving
- 1910s – 1920s girl in pink bonnet with red ribbon, house, trees, and lawn in background
- 1910s – 1920s girl in pink dress and bonnet, boy in velvet sailor suit, brick border, heart insert
- 1910s – 1920s girl in pink dress, small heart card
- 1910s – 1920s girl in white dress looking over right shoulder, sunflowers with child heads, lace overlay, scraps
- 1910s – 1920s girl in yellow hoop dress, pantaloons, two dolls
- 1910s – 1920s girl with ringlet curls
- 1910s – 1920s heart card with farm house and front yard, pink floral border
- 1910s – 1920s heart card with four red birds, shield insert
- 1910s – 1920s heart card, girl in green polka-dotted dress writing on paper, candle in background, heart top and square bottom
- 1910s – 1920s heart card, girl in light pink dress, lace overlay, applied scraps of girl in old-fashioned dress and basket scraps
- 1910s – 1920s large couple on lace front, lily of the valley
- 1910s – 1920s sailor boy and girl with lace overlay
- 1910s – 1920s yellow heart with four bluebirds, flowers, shield insert

Whitney cards dated 1917, boxed sets in George Whitney Sample Book, lots numbered

- 1917 bluebirds and nest, no. 40
- 1917 boy and girl under green umbrella, raining across, rectangle card
- 1917 boy bowing to girl in red dress, blue floral border, no. 196, 3 designs, 12 in a box
- 1917 boy in overalls, girl in red cap looking at door, heart-shaped card
- 1917 boy in red cap delivering card by a door, no. 40
- 1917 boy in red cap sending a valentine, no. 43
- 1917 boy leaning hand on chin sitting under a tree, circular bench with a broken heart, heart-shaped card
- 1917 boy proposing to girl, no. 39
- 1917 boy with big brown hat, three geese, red floral poppies on top, square card
- 1917 child with red winter outfit, paper lace, floral border, scraps, no. 57E
- 1917 couple at golden door, no. 39
- 1917 couple blue border, applied scrap, no. 48
- 1917 couple by wooden fence, no. 42
- 1917 couple under umbrella, no. 42
- 1917 couple with suitcase, no. 42
- 1917 cut out fold open, boy, green door opens revealing girl, part of no. 182 group, 72 designs in box
- 1917 die-cut angel, sealing wax, forget-me-nots, and valentine letter, part of no. 190, 12 in a box
- 1917 die-cut boy and girl with floral bouquet, "Yours truly," no. 267, 6 designs, 50 per box
- 1917 die-cut boy and girl, " Some sparkler, eh?," no. 267, 6 designs, 50 per box
- 1917 die-cut boy and sled, part of no. 181 group, 12 designs in box
- 1917 die-cut boy carrying huge salt shaker, part of

Chapter 10: 1910 – 1919 Flat Cards

no. 181 group, 12 designs in box

- 1917 die-cut fold out boy leaves valentines under door, door reveals girl, no. 182
- 1917 die-cut girl sitting on boy's lap, no. 267, 6 designs, 50 in box
- 1917 die-cut telephone directory, part of no. 181 group, 12 designs in box
- 1917 die-cut girl and farm box, blind man's bluff, no. 267, 6 designs, 50 in box
- 1917 die-cut girl in heart wearing old-fashioned dress and knitting, no. 267, 6 designs, 50 in box
- 1917 fan scene, lace, flowers, scraps, no. 52E
- 1917 fishing boat scene, no. 51E
- 1917 fold open tent, girl buying hearts, part of no. 182 group, 72 designs in box
- 1917 girl and boy wearing prairie and farm clothes, rectangular card, no. 196, 3 designs, 12 in a box
- 1917 girl at desk, no. 39
- 1917 girl holding flowers, heart-shaped card, part of no. 190, 12 in a box
- 1917 girl in a bonnet, boy from behind, blue roses, small rectangular card
- 1917 girl in a swing, no. 40
- 1917 girl in pink dress with bow and box, rectangular card
- 1917 girl in red coat, snow scene, and house beyond, part of no. 181 group, 12 designs in box
- 1917 girl making a valentine, no. 40
- 1917 girl on path, no. 39
- 1917 girl with Asian parasol, no. 43
- 1917 girl's profile with headband, rectangular card, part of no. 196, 3 designs, 12 per box
- 1917 heart-shaped fold open, boy on tree bench, hand on chin, part of no. 182 group, 72 designs in box
- 1917 heart, boy holds girl's hand, wearing winter outfits, part of no. 190, 12 in a box
- 1917 heart, motorcycle couple, one girl inside card, square bottom, farm scene in background, 12 in a box
- 1917 heart, motorcycle couple, square bottom, heart-shaped top, farm scene, one of a set of 12 sold per box
- 1917 hearts, "Accept this Token," no. 263, 12 designs, 50 per box
- 1917 hearts, "Best Thoughts of Love," no. 263, 12 designs, 50 per box
- 1917 hearts, "Cupid's Offering," no. 261, 12 designs, 50 per box
- 1917 hearts, "Golden Arrows of Love," no. 263, 12 designs, 50 per box
- 1917 hearts, "Love's Tributes," no. 261, 12 designs, 50 per box
- 1917 hearts, "My Heart's Gift," no. 261, 12 designs, 50 per box
- 1917 hearts, "Sincere Regards," no. 263, 12 designs, 50 per box
- 1917 hearts, "To Greet Thee," no. 261, 12 designs, 50 per box
- 1917 hearts, "To My Valentine," no. 261, 12 designs, 50 per box
- 1917 hearts, "Whispers of True Love," no. 263, 12 designs, 50 per box
- 1917 hearts, "With Loving Thoughts," no. 263, 12 designs, 50 per box
- 1917 hearts, "With Sincere Love," no. 261, 12 designs, 50 per box
- 1917 large heart top and square bottom, goose boy, no. 41
- 1917 large heart top and square bottom, sidecar, no. 41
- 1917 large heart top and square bottom, sweetheart bargain day store, no. 41
- 1917 large heart top and square bottom, telephone, no. 41
- 1917 large heart, child couple under umbrella with floral border, no. 46
- 1917 large heart, floral border, boy with big hat, no. 46
- 1917 large heart, lace, flowers, girl in boat, no. 48
- 1917 large rectangular card, child on phone, long leaf shaped lace, floral border, scraps, layered, no. 57E
- 1917 large rectangular card, children, parrot border, part of no. 185 group, 8 designs, 12 in box
- 1917 large square card with diamond-shaped doily, floral corners, farm scene, no. 51E
- 1917 large square card with fern-shaped lace paper, no. 51E
- 1917 large square card, silver scroll lace, interior scene, window seat, floral corners, scraps, no. 55E
- 1917 large valentine, two children on swing, silhouette figures on bottom, heart vignette, no. 149
- 1917 old farm girl, lace in leaf shape, flower scraps, no. 52E
- 1917 outdoor scene, paper lace, hearts, no. 53E
- 1917 red heart cards, no. 274
- 1917 small hearts, boy in overalls, no. 268, 6 designs, 50 in box
- 1917 small hearts, cupid holding roses in box, no. 268, 6 designs, 50 in box
- 1917 small hearts, cupid with blue ribbon, no. 268, 6 designs, 50 in box
- 1917 small hearts, cupid with eyes cast down low, no. 268, 6 designs, 50 in box
- 1917 small hearts, girl in bonnet, stick fishing rod catching a heart, no. 268, 6 designs, 50 in box
- 1917 small hearts, cupid with cap, no. 268, 6 designs, 50 in box
- 1917 small square cutout card, opens to child on high chair, part of no. 181 group, 12 designs in box

- 1917 square card, gold accent, two children eating ice cream, boy in sailor suit, bistro table
- 1917 square card with sunbonnet girl, hearts, blue rose border, no. 267, 6 designs, 50 in box
- 1917 square lace doily, girl in center, scraps around doily, part of no. 185, 8 designs, 12 in a box

- 1917 sunbonnet girl in heart, no. 39
- 1917 two cupids and door knocker, no. 43
- 1918 angel with red heart and blue forget-me-not flowers, rectangular card
- 1919 boy in blue dress catching butterflies, heart shaped

Exact years in captions are original sender/receiver dates.

Die-cut with easel valentine; publisher: Raphael Tuck; printer markings: Raphael Tuck & Sons, Ltd., Publishers to Their Majesties the King and the Queen and her Majesty Queen Alexandra (widowed Queen of Edward VII 1910 – 1925) Raphael Tuck trademark easel, Printed in Germany; circa 1910s; no notice of copyright. $35.00 – 65.00.

Die-cut with easel valentine; publisher: Raphael Tuck; printer markings: Raphael Tuck & Sons, Ltd., Printed in Germany, Raphael Tuck trademark easel; circa 1910s; no notice of copyright. $35.00 – 65.00.

Die-cut fold open valentine; unknown publisher; printer markings: "E"; circa 1900s – 1910s; no notice of copyright. $15.00 – 25.00.

1910

Flat valentine; anonymous publisher; printer markings: none; 1910; no notice of copyright. $5.00 – 8.00.

Fold open valentine; anonymous publisher; printer markings: none; 1910; no notice of copyright. $4.00 – 6.00.

Die-cut fold out valentine; anonymous publisher; printer markings: none; circa 1910s; no notice of copyright. $5.00 – 8.00.

1911

Fold open valentine; anonymous publisher; printer markings: none; 1911; no notice of copyright. $5.00 – 10.00.

Hanging valentine, lace, tassels, and air-brushed design; publisher: A.C. McClurg & Sons; valentine box markings: Chicago Illinois; 1911; no notice of copyright. $10.00 – 18.00.

Die-cut fold out valentine; anonymous publisher; printer markings: none; circa 1910s; no notice of copyright. $5.00 – 8.00.

1912

Die-cut valentine; anonymous publisher; printer markings: none; 1912; no notice of copyright. $10.00 – 18.00.

Fold open valentine; anonymous publisher; printer markings: none; 1912; no notice of copyright. $5.00 – 8.00.

Fold open valentine; anonymous publisher; printer markings: none; 1910s; no notice of copyright. $6.00 – 10.00.

Fold open valentine; anonymous publisher; printer markings: none; circa 1910s; no notice of copyright. $4.00 – 8.00.

Chapter 10: 1910 – 1919 Flat Cards

Flat fold open valentine; anonymous publisher; printer markings: none; 1912; no notice of copyright. $6.00 – 10.00.

1913

Fold open valentine; anonymous publisher; printer markings: none; 1913; no notice of copyright. $12.00 – 18.00.

Fold open valentine; anonymous publisher; printer markings: none; circa 1913; no notice of copyright. $5.00 – 8.00.

Fold open valentine; anonymous publisher; printer markings: none; 1913; no notice of copyright. $5.00 – 8.00.

Fold open valentine; anonymous publisher; printer markings: none; circa 1913; no notice of copyright. $5.00 – 8.00.

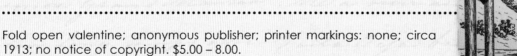

Fold open valentine; anonymous publisher; printer markings: none; 1913; no notice of copyright. $6.00 – 10.00.

1915

Stand-up die-cut with easel support; publisher: Raphael Tuck & Sons; printer markings: Printed in Saxony; 1915; no notice of copyright. $30.00 – 40.00.

1916

Fold open valentine; anonymous publisher; printer markings: none; 1916; no notice of copyright. $4.00 – 6.00.

1917

Fold open valentine; unknown publisher; printer markings: "A"; circa 1917; no notice of copyright. $5.00 – 8.00.

Fold out valentine; anonymous publisher; printer markings: none; circa 1917 – 1920s; no notice of copyright. $6.00 – 9.00.

Fold open valentine; anonymous publisher; printer markings: none; circa 1917; no notice of copyright. $5.00 – 8.00.

Die-cut scrap with paper lace; anonymous publisher; printer markings: none; circa 1900s – 1910s; no notice of copyright. $4.00 – 6.00.

Fold open valentine; anonymous publisher; printer markings: none; circa 1910s; no notice of copyright. $5.00 – 8.00.

Die-cut scrap with paper lace; anonymous publisher; printer markings: none; circa 1900s – 1910s; no notice of copyright. $4.00 – 6.00.

Fold open valentine; anonymous publisher; printer markings: none; circa 1910s; no notice of copyright. $5.00 – 8.00.

Fold open valentine; anonymous publisher; printer markings: none; circa 1910s; no notice of copyright. $5.00 – 8.00.

Fold open valentine; anonymous publisher; printer markings: none; circa 1910s; no notice of copyright. $5.00 – 8.00.

Fold open valentine; anonymous publisher; printer markings: none; circa 1910s; no notice of copyright. $10.00 – 15.00.

Chapter 10: 1910 – 1919 *Flat Cards*

Fold open valentine; anonymous publisher; printer markings: none; circa 1910s – 1920s; no notice of copyright. $6.00 – 9.00.

Mechanical stand-up valentine, arm and eyes move; unknown publisher; printer markings: "E"; circa 1917 – 1919; no notice of copyright. $20.00 – 30.00.

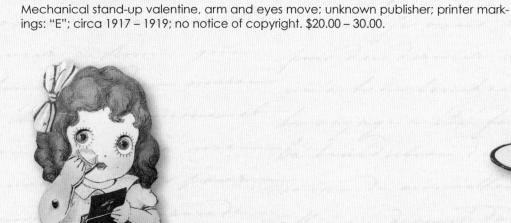

Mechanical stand-up valentine, arm and eyes move; unknown publisher; printer markings: "E"; circa 1917 – 1919; no notice of copyright. $20.00 – 30.00.

Mechanical stand-up valentine, arm and eyes move; anonymous publisher; printer markings: none; circa 1917 – 1919; no notice of copyright. $20.00 – 25.00.

Flat valentine; anonymous publisher; printer markings: none; circa 1910s; no notice of copyright. $8.00 – 12.00.

Flat valentine with side easels; anonymous publisher; printer markings: none; circa 1910s – 1920s; no notice of copyright. $10.00 – 15.00.

Flat valentine with side easels; anonymous publisher; printer markings: none; circa 1910s – 1920s; no notice of copyright. $7.00 – 10.00.

Fold open valentine; anonymous publisher; printer markings: Made in U.S.A.; circa 1910s – 1930s; no notice of copyright. $6.00 – 9.00.

Fold open valentine; anonymous publisher; printer markings: Printed in U.S.AM.; circa 1910s – 1930s; no notice of copyright. $6.00 – 9.00.

Fold open valentine; anonymous publisher; printer markings: none; circa 1910s – 1930s; no notice of copyright. $6.00 – 9.00.

Fold open valentine; anonymous publisher; printer markings: none; circa 1910s – 1930s; no notice of copyright. $6.00 – 9.00.

Fold open valentine; anonymous publisher; printer markings: none; circa 1910s – 1930s; no notice of copyright. $6.00 – 9.00.

Fold open valentine; anonymous publisher; printer markings: Made in U.S.A.; circa 1910s – 1930s; no notice of copyright. $6.00 – 9.00.

1918

Die-cut fold out valentine; anonymous publisher; printer markings: none; 1918; no notice of copyright. $5.00 – 8.00.

Die-cut fold out valentine; anonymous publisher; printer markings: none; circa 1918; no notice of copyright. $5.00 – 8.00.

Die-cut fold out valentine; anonymous publisher; printer markings: Printed in Germany; circa 1918; no notice of copyright. $5.00 – 8.00.

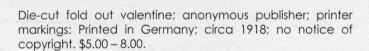

TO MY VALENTINE

Die-cut fold out valentine; anonymous publisher; printer markings: Printed in Germany; circa 1918; no notice of copyright. $5.00 – 8.00.

TO MY VALENTINE

TO MY VALENTINE

Die-cut fold out valentine; anonymous publisher; printer markings: Printed in Germany; circa 1918; no notice of copyright. $5.00 – 8.00.

Die-cut fold out valentine; anonymous publisher; printer markings: Printed in Germany; circa 1918; no notice of copyright. $5.00 – 8.00.

Die-cut fold out valentine; anonymous publisher; printer markings: Printed in Germany; circa 1918; no notice of copyright. $5.00 – 8.00.

Die-cut fold out valentine; anonymous publisher; printer markings: Printed in Germany; circa 1918; no notice of copyright. $5.00 – 8.00.

Die-cut fold out valentine; anonymous publisher; printer markings: Printed in Germany; circa 1918; no notice of copyright. $5.00 – 8.00.

Die-cut fold out valentine; anonymous publisher; printer markings: none; circa 1918; no notice of copyright. $5.00 – 8.00.

1919

Fold open valentine; anonymous publisher; printer markings: none; circa 1919; no notice of copyright. $5.00 – 8.00.

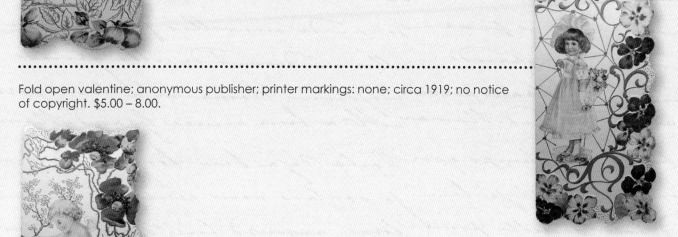

Fold open valentine; anonymous publisher; printer markings: none; circa 1919; no notice of copyright. $5.00 – 8.00.

Fold open valentine; anonymous publisher; printer markings: none; circa 1919; no notice of copyright. $5.00 – 8.00.

Fold open valentine; anonymous publisher; printer markings: none; circa 1900s – 1910s; no notice of copyright. $5.00 – 8.00.

Fold open valentine; anonymous publisher; printer markings: none; circa 1900s – 1910s; no notice of copyright. $5.00 – 8.00.

Chapter 10: 1910 – 1919 *Flat Cards*

Fold open valentine; anonymous publisher; printer markings: none; circa 1900s – 1910s; no notice of copyright. $5.00 – 8.00.

Fold open valentine; anonymous publisher; printer markings: none; 1919; no notice of copyright. $10.00 – 15.00.

Fold open valentine; anonymous publisher (possibly Whitney); printer markings: none; 1919 (also recorded in 1917 Whitney Salesman Sample Book); no notice of copyright. $5.00 – 8.00.

Die-cut valentine; anonymous publisher; printer markings: none; circa 1910s – 1920s; no notice of copyright. $10.00 – 20.00.

Small booklet valentine; anonymous publisher; printer markings: none; circa 1910s; no notice of copyright. $4.00 – 8.00.

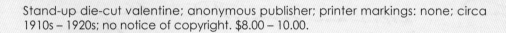

Stand-up die-cut valentine with easel; anonymous publisher; printer markings: Printed in Saxony; circa 1910s; no notice of copyright. $8.00 – 15.00.

Stand-up die-cut valentine; anonymous publisher; printer markings: none; circa 1910s – 1920s; no notice of copyright. $8.00 – 10.00.

Stand-up die-cut valentine; anonymous publisher; printer markings: Germany on front, 2 on back; circa 1900s – 1910s; no notice of copyright. $10.00 – 20.00.

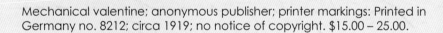

Mechanical valentine; anonymous publisher; printer markings: Printed in Germany no. 8212; circa 1919; no notice of copyright. $15.00 – 25.00.

Die-cut valentine; anonymous publisher; printer markings: none; circa 1900s – 1910s; no notice of copyright. $5.00 – 10.00.

Flat die-cut valentine; anonymous publisher; printer markings: none; circa 1900s – 1910s; no notice of copyright. $8.00 – 10.00.

Flat die-cut valentine; anonymous publisher; printer markings: none; circa 1910s; no notice of copyright. $8.00 – 15.00.

Flat valentine; anonymous publisher; printer markings: none; circa 1910s; no notice of copyright. $4.00 – 8.00.

Flat valentine; anonymous publisher; printer markings: none; circa 1910s; no notice of copyright. $4.00 – 8.00.

Fold out valentine; anonymous publisher; printer markings: none; circa 1910s; no notice of copyright. $6.00 – 10.00.

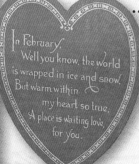

Fold out valentines; anonymous publisher; printer markings: none; circa 1910s; no notice of copyright. $6.00 – 10.00.

Flat die-cut valentine; anonymous publisher; printer markings: Germany; circa 1900s – 1920s; no notice of copyright. $4.00 – 6.00.

Flat die-cut valentine; anonymous publisher; printer markings: Printed in Germany; circa 1900s – 1920s; no notice of copyright. $6.00 – 8.00.

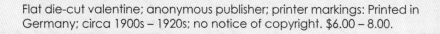

Flat die-cut valentine; anonymous publisher; printer markings: Printed in Germany; circa 1900s – 1920s; no notice of copyright. $6.00 – 8.00.

Flat die-cut valentine; anonymous publisher; printer markings: Printed in Germany; circa 1910s – 1920s; no notice of copyright. $8.00 – 10.00.

Flat die-cut valentine; anonymous publisher; printer markings: Printed in Germany; circa 1910s – 1920s; no notice of copyright. $8.00 – 10.00.

Flat die-cut valentine; anonymous publisher; printer markings: none; circa 1910s; no notice of copyright. $6.00 – 8.00.

Die-cut fold out valentine; anonymous publisher; printer markings: Printed in Germany; circa 1900s – 1920s; no notice of copyright. $6.00 – 10.00.

Flat die-cut valentine; anonymous publisher; printer markings: none; circa 1910s; no notice of copyright. $8.00 – 15.00.

Flat die-cut valentine; anonymous publisher; printer markings: none; circa 1900s – 1910s; no notice of copyright. $8.00 – 10.00.

Stand-up die-cut scrap valentine; anonymous publisher; printer markings: Printed in Germany; circa 1900s – 1910s; no notice of copyright. $8.00 – 15.00.

Flat die-cut valentine; anonymous publisher; printer markings: none; circa 1910s – 1920s; no notice of copyright. $8.00 – 10.00.

Chapter 11
1910 ~ 1919
Fold Down Cards

Fold down valentines continued to be made and printed in Germany through the decade. As American greeting card manufactures developed and grew their businesses, they had much to compete with against German experience, artistry, and the affordably priced products. American card manufacturers began making products that lacked the artistic expertise of German chromolithography. This might explain why there are so many mass-produced German cards in collections. Cards appear to have inferior quality designs, bleeding inks, and lower quality paper around wartime. Some American manufacturers used German scraps to create new cards. The later cards were an artistic achievement given lesser quality materials and inexperienced techniques. They would continue to be a favorite in the years before and after World War I.

Anonymously Published Card
Markings Indicating Place of Manufacture or Printing

- "Germany"
- "Made in Germany"
- "Printed in Germany"

Types of Valentines Illustrated

- Fold down cards
- Small die-cut stand-up cards

Design Features Illustrated

- Chromolithograph scraps
- Deep and rich chromolithograph colors
- Dresden gold or silver scrap ornament
- Heavy paper
- Large heart designs
- Scrolling die-cut card backs
- Shiny chromolithograph scraps
- Small ball of folded open tissue paper honeycomb at base of card
- Textured paper

Subjects Illustrated

- Angels and cupids
- Architecture
- Automobiles
- Baskets of flowers
- Birds
- Bouquets
- Boys in old-fashioned attire
- Cartoon-style children
- Dogs
- Garden themes
- Girls in old-fashioned attire
- Hearts
- Roses meaning in 1857: beauty [115]
- Telephones
- Violets meaning in 1857: modesty [116]

Exact years in captions are original sender/receiver dates.

Fold down valentine; anonymous publisher; printer markings: none; 1910s; no notice of copyright. $15.00 – 25.00.

Fold down valentine; unknown publisher; printer markings: "E"; circa 1910s – 1920s; no notice of copyright. $8.00 – 15.00.

Fold down valentine; anonymous publisher; printer markings: none; circa 1910s – 1920s; no notice of copyright. $8.00 – 15.00.

Fold down valentine; anonymous publisher; printer markings: Printed in Germany; circa 1900s – 1910s; no notice of copyright. $6.00 – 10.00.

Fold down valentine; anonymous publisher; printer markings: Germany; circa 1900s – 1910s; no notice of copyright. $8.00 – 12.00.

Fold down valentine; anonymous publisher; printer markings: Printed in Germany; circa 1900s – 1910s; no notice of copyright. $6.00 – 10.00.

Fold down valentine; anonymous publisher; printer markings: Printed in Germany; circa 1910s – 1920s; no notice of copyright. $8.00 – 12.00.

Fold down valentine; anonymous publisher; printer markings: Germany; circa 1900s – 1920s; no notice of copyright. $10.00 – 20.00.

1910

Fold down valentine; anonymous publisher; printer markings: none; 1910; no notice of copyright. $45.00 – 55.00.

Fold down valentine; anonymous publisher; printer markings: Printed in Germany; circa 1900s – 1910s; no notice of copyright. $40.00 – 50.00.

1912

Fold down valentine; anonymous publisher; printer markings: Made in Germany; circa 1912; no notice of copyright. $8.00 – 15.00.

Fold down valentine; anonymous publisher; printer markings: Germany; 1912; no notice of copyright. $8.00 – 10.00.

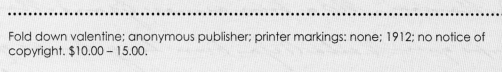

Fold down valentine; anonymous publisher; printer markings: none; 1912; no notice of copyright. $10.00 – 15.00.

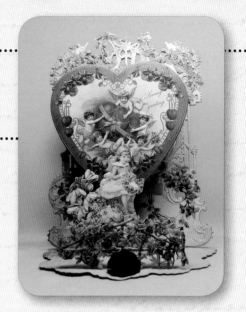

1915

Fold down valentine; anonymous publisher; printer markings: Germany; 1915; no notice of copyright. $50.00 – 55.00.

1916

Fold down valentine; anonymous publisher; printer markings: none; 1916; no notice of copyright. $6.00 – 10.00.

Fold down valentine; anonymous publisher; printer markings: none; circa 1910s – early 1920s; no notice of copyright. $12.00 – 20.00.

Fold down valentine; anonymous publisher; printer markings: none; circa 1910s – early 1920s; no notice of copyright. $12.00 – 15.00.

Fold down valentine; anonymous publisher; printer markings: none; circa 1910s – early 1920s; no notice of copyright. $6.00 – 10.00.

Fold down valentine; anonymous publisher; printer markings: none; circa 1910s – 1920s; no notice of copyright. $6.00 – 10.00.

Fold down valentine; anonymous publisher; printer markings: none; circa 1910s – early 1920s; no notice of copyright. $12.00 – 15.00.

Fold down valentine; anonymous publisher; printer markings: none; circa 1910s – 1920s; no notice of copyright. $6.00 – 10.00.

Chapter 12
1920 - 1929
Flat Cards

Germany and the United States continued to make valentines for the American market after the Great War. World War I would have historically made it difficult for any printing business in Germany to thrive and even survive. Germany faced deep financial problems after World War I when they were forced to pay reparations. A crippling economy would lead to hyperinflation during the 1920s. German printed cards are a mystery to collectors. Many period valentines are unmarked leaving us to assume they were made either in America or elsewhere without established certainty. Many more were marked "Printed in Germany," but it is not certain if they were made by German firms for the American market or American companies choosing to take advantage of skilled German printing techniques. Both World War I and II brought about the unfortunate bombing of cities, resulting in much material destruction and loss of life. Whatever the origin of these cards, their background is somewhat of a mystery. It is certain they continue to appear in America no matter what their true origin or the impact of the Great War.

Printing and paper quality begins to change with cards of this period. American greeting card publishers begin to advance in their technique and artistry. Since many of these artistic examples are unmarked and indicate no company, artist, or printer on either side of the Atlantic, they continue to baffle and intrigue us through time. We cannot be sure any card was designed in America or in Germany by way of maker, manufacturer, or printer. There is no historical certainty or indication in manufacture except for those made by the largest companies.

Valentines took on a more personalized tone in the 1920s. For the first time makers made sweetheart themed cards or cards that specialized for individuals such as Mother, Dad, Baby, and Teacher. New designs included ladies and gentlemen in colonial dress, floral designs, relief prints, and die stamping in silver and gold. Beautiful lined envelopes and colored landscapes made Art Deco valentines something special.[117] The American valentine industry had created a card that had reflected a movement away from European customs and traditional designs to reflect a new American spirit. While it took card makers some time to be able to perfect better printing, the new theme came to reflect American culture.

Important Valentine Manufacturers, Publishers, and Printers

Hallmark Greeting Card Company
- Hallmark of Kansas City, Missouri, began business in 1920 as Hall Brothers.[118]

Types of Valentines Illustrated

- Die-cut valentines
- Flat valentines
- Flat valentines with side easels
- Fold down tent shaped cards
- Fold open valentines
- Fold out cards with tent shaped fronts
- Tent cards

Design Features Illustrated

- Chromolithograph scraps
- Paper lace

Subjects Illustrated

- Anthropomorphism
- Art Deco themes
- Bicycles
- Birds
- Bouquets
- Cats
- Child couples
- Children in outdoor activities
- Children playing
- Dogs
- Doves
- Flowers
- Giving hearts
- Google-eyed children

- Hearts
- Love letters
- Musicians
- Roses meaning in 1857: beauty[119]
- Sheep
- Targets with hearts as bull's eyes

Published Cards Not Illustrated

Carrington, Chicago, Illinois
Cards have a value of $5.00 – 15.00 each.
Trademarks or logos: tree outline with E, H, or A inside and H in a circle.

- 1920s "C," possibly Carrington, Made in USA, fold out, two flappers wearing hats
- 1920s "C," possibly Carrington, Made in USA, fold out, two flappers, girl and boy
- 1920s boy and girl at fence
- 1920s boy and girl weightlifting, heart-shaped card
- 1920s couple at the beach
- 1920s Dutch couple
- 1920s flowers, small card
- 1920s girl chased by boy
- 1920s girl in field wearing a large hat
- 1920s girl on moon, boy with heart lantern
- 1920s girl with a wreath of flowers
- 1920s girl with embroidered hankie and birdcage, Made in USA
- 1920s girl with parasol sitting on a bench
- 1920s honeymoon speedster, fold down
- 1920s sailor boy
- 1920s, boy and girl, "Say when"
- 1921 Art Deco style woman in gown with bouquet
- 1924 girl dunking valentine in sugar, Katz artist, Carrington publisher, copyright 1924
- 1920s – 1930s Art Deco style couple kissing
- 1920s – 1930s boy and girl at a gate
- 1920s – 1930s boy dressed as sailor
- 1920s – 1930s clown behind bars, cutout front, Made in USA
- 1920s – 1930s clown in blue suit, cutout front, Made in USA
- 1920s – 1930s clown in red suit serenading on lute, lace overlay, girl and heart applied scraps, Made in USA
- 1920s – 1930s clown in yellow polka-dot suit, Made in USA
- 1920s – 1930s cut out card with tent fold down front, boy wearing red sweater and blue knickers mailing valentine, house and girl in background, Made in USA
- 1920s – 1930s cut out card with tent fold down front, child in boat, boy swimming, Made in USA
- 1920s – 1930s cut out card with tent fold down front,

girl in yellow dress and boy in blue sailor suit under red umbrella, sad man in background, Made in USA
- 1920s – 1930s cut out front card of girl in yellow dress with broken heart, inside boy in red sweater and blue knickers, Made in USA
- 1920s – 1930s girl at a heart gate
- 1920s – 1930s girl in red dress and green apron holding heart, lace overlay, applied scraps, Made in USA
- 1920s – 1930s girl in yellow dress, old-fashioned hat, lace overlay, applied scraps, Made in USA
- 1920s – 1930s red heart cutout front, girl in purple dress, Made in USA

Miscellaneous Manufacturers
Cards have a value of $5.00 – 10.00 each.
1920s – 1940s girl and boy police, fold out "better beat my time," Made in U.S.A.

Whitney
Cards have a value of $5.00 – 15.00 each.
- 1920s ballerina and clown
- 1920s bluebirds and pink flowers
- 1920s boy and girl in garden with wall between them, heart-shaped card
- 1920s boy and girl riding bicycles, cut out shape
- 1920s boy in eighteenth century clothing boxing, heart shape
- 1920s boy in brown hat with dog
- 1920s boy with heart semaphore flags
- 1920s boy, girl, and cupid in center oval, heart-shaped card
- 1920s child holding heart, gold and blue flowers
- 1920s child with green suit, gold daisies in white, green, and blue
- 1920s couple in snow, heart shape
- 1920s couple inside heart
- 1920s couple looking to the left, heart-shaped card
- 1920s couple on a bench
- 1920s couple on globe, medium sized rectangular card
- 1920s couple sleigh riding
- 1920s couple with umbrella, heart-shaped card
- 1920s cupids and a "Just Married" trunk, heart top and square bottom
- 1920s cut out style of boy and girl, "Birds and Flowers"
- 1920s dog in heart
- 1920s girl and boy sitting in flower field
- 1920s girl in big white hat, purple and red hearts
- 1920s girl in blue dress holding out her skirt

- 1920s girl in blue dress drinking tea with doll
- 1920s girl in blue dress with straw cloche helmet hat, cutout shape
- 1920s girl in gray hat, blue and pink flowers, rectangular shape
- 1920s girl in green checked dress
- 1920s girl in hat looking over her right shoulder
- 1920s girl in pink coat with lace overlay
- 1920s girl in purple dress
- 1920s girl in red coat with white muff, heart-shaped card
- 1920s girl in red and white hat, small rectangular card
- 1920s girl in yellow dress with bouquet
- 1920s girl in yellow dress, lace overlay
- 1920s girl reading valentine, lace with butterfly embossing, dog, floral and basket scraps
- 1920s girl with lambs on a farm
- 1920s girl with purple dress and red hat
- 1920s girl with red hair, gold heart, ivory lace in heart shape
- 1920s girl with ringlet curls
- 1920s girl with yellow dress, purple flowers, Art Deco heart design
- 1920s pink heart with girl in purple dress, heart-shaped card
- 1920s sailor boy in heart
- 1920s small red heart-shaped card with girl in a dress holding flowers
- 1923 red haired girl with purple side bow, floral and mushroom border, heart-shaped card
- 1925 girl in purple dress, bouquet, gold heart, "Be my Valentine...My Words are Brief," postcard
- 1925 girl with red winter hat, white trim and pompom, red scarf, ivory embossed lace, pansy and

- heart scraps, heart-shaped card
- 1927 dark haired girl, yellow dress, small rectangular card
- 1927 girl in blue coat, little girl in red coat, muff, lace overlay, butterfly, purple scraps, heart top and square bottom
- 1927 girl in center, dog, basket, and heart scraps, lace overlay, heart-shaped card
- 1927 girl in purple dress, big red hat, small rectangular card
- 1928 and 1929 red heart with gold, girl in red dress holding pink heart, red border with white mesh design, small rectangular card
- 1928 black haired girl, orange checked dress, yellow flower, red heart border, heart-shaped card
- 1928 girl in pink dress with doll and four hearts, small rectangular card
- 1929 and 1930 boy in sailor suit looking back over his shoulder, blue-green, white, and red border, small rectangular shape
- 1929 boy and girl reclining in flowers, red, blue, white, and gold border, small rectangle
- 1920s – 1930s boy with elephant
- 1920s – 1930s child in heart
- 1920s – 1930s farmer boy and girl with daisies, rectangular card
- 1920s – 1930s girl in yellow dress standing with boy wearing a green checked top and socks, small rectangular card
- 1920s – 1930s girl walking dog in the wind
- 1920s – 1930s small couple in field picking flowers

Exact years in captions are original sender/receiver dates.

1920

Flat valentine; anonymous publisher; printer markings: Printed in Germany; 1920; no notice of copyright. $6.00 – 9.00.

Flat valentine; anonymous publisher; printer markings: Printed in Germany; circa 1920s; no notice of copyright. $8.00 – 12.00.

Fold out valentine; anonymous publisher; printer markings: none; circa 1920s; no notice of copyright. $7.00 – 10.00.

Fold out valentine; anonymous publisher; printer markings: Germany; circa 1910s – 1920s; no notice of copyright. $7.00 – 10.00.

Fold out valentine; anonymous publisher; printer markings: Germany; circa 1910s – 1920s; no notice of copyright. $7.00 – 10.00.

Fold out valentine; anonymous publisher; printer markings: Series No. 159, 12 designs Valentine Cut-outs; circa 1920s; no notice of copyright. $6.00 – 9.00.

Fold out valentine; anonymous publisher; printer markings: Series No. 315 Valentine Cut Outs 12 designs; circa 1920s; no notice of copyright. $6.00 – 9.00.

Fold out valentine; anonymous publisher; printer markings: Series No. 316 Valentine Cut Outs 12 designs; circa 1920s; no notice of copyright. $6.00 – 9.00.

Fold out valentine; anonymous publisher; printer markings: Series No. 179 Valentine Novelties 12 designs; circa 1920s; no notice of copyright. $6.00 – 9.00.

Fold out valentine; anonymous publisher; printer markings: Series No. 156 Valentine Cut Outs 12 designs; circa 1920s; no notice of copyright. $6.00 – 9.00.

Fold out valentine; anonymous publisher; printer markings: Series No. 315 Valentine Cut Outs 12 designs; circa 1920s; no notice of copyright. $6.00 – 9.00.

Fold out valentine; anonymous publisher; printer markings: Series No. 179 Valentine Novelties 12 designs; circa 1920s; no notice of copyright. $6.00 – 9.00.

Fold out valentine; anonymous publisher; printer markings: none; circa 1910s – 1920s; no notice of copyright. $5.00 – 8.00.

Fold out valentine; anonymous publisher; printer markings: none; 1920; no notice of copyright. $6.00 – 9.00.

Fold out valentine; anonymous publisher; printer markings: none; circa 1910s – 1920s; no notice of copyright. $5.00 – 8.00.

Fold out valentine; anonymous publisher; printer markings: none; circa 1910s – 1920s; no notice of copyright. $5.00 – 8.00.

Fold out valentine (inside view of open card) showing children before and after playing with their pea shooters; anonymous publisher; printer markings: Printed in Germany; circa 1910s – 1920s; no notice of copyright. $5.00 – 8.00.

Fold out valentine (front view) revealing the closed cover view of children playing with their pea shooters.

1923

Fold out valentine; anonymous publisher; printer markings: Series No. 331 Valentine Cut Outs 12 designs; 1923; no notice of copyright. $6.00 – 9.00.

Fold out valentine; anonymous publisher; printer markings: Series No. 277 Valentine Cut Outs 12 designs; circa 1920s; no notice of copyright. $6.00 – 9.00.

Fold out valentine; anonymous publisher; printer markings: Series No. 265 Valentine Cut Outs 12 designs; circa 1920s; no notice of copyright. $6.00 – 9.00.

Fold out valentine; anonymous publisher; printer markings: Printed in Germany; circa 1910s – 1920s; no notice of copyright. $5.00 – 8.00.

Fold out valentine; anonymous publisher; printer markings: none; circa 1920s; no notice of copyright. $6.00 – 9.00.

Fold out valentine; anonymous publisher; printer markings: Series No. 277 Valentine Cut Outs 12 designs; circa 1920s; no notice of copyright. $6.00 – 9.00.

Fold out valentine; anonymous publisher; printer markings: Series No. 328 Valentine Cut Outs 12 designs; circa 1920s; no notice of copyright. $6.00 – 9.00.

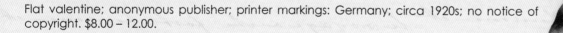

Flat valentine; anonymous publisher; printer markings: Germany; circa 1920s; no notice of copyright. $8.00 – 12.00.

Flat valentine; anonymous publisher; printer markings: Printed in Germany; circa 1920s; no notice of copyright. $10.00 – 15.00.

Chapter 12: 1920 – 1929 Flat Cards

Flat valentine; anonymous publisher; printer markings: none; circa 1920s; no notice of copyright. $8.00 – 12.00.

Fold out valentine; anonymous publisher; printer markings: none; circa 1910s – 1920s; no notice of copyright. $5.00 – 8.00.

Fold out valentine; anonymous publisher; printer markings: none; circa 1910s – 1920s; no notice of copyright. $5.00 – 8.00.

Fold out valentine; anonymous publisher; printer markings: none; circa 1910s – 1920s; no notice of copyright. $5.00 – 8.00.

Fold out valentine; anonymous publisher; printer markings: Printed in Germany; circa 1910s – 1920s; no notice of copyright. $5.00 – 8.00.

Fold out valentine; anonymous publisher; printer markings: Printed in Germany; circa 1910s – 1920s; no notice of copyright. $5.00 – 8.00.

Fold out valentine; anonymous publisher; printer markings: Printed in Germany; circa 1910s – 1920s; no notice of copyright. $5.00 – 8.00.

Fold out valentine; anonymous publisher; printer markings: none; circa 1910s – 1920s; no notice of copyright. $6.00 – 9.00.

Fold out valentine; anonymous publisher; printer markings: Printed in Germany; circa 1910s – 1920s; no notice of copyright. $5.00 – 8.00.

Fold out valentine; anonymous publisher; printer markings: none; circa 1910s – 1920s; no notice of copyright. $6.00 – 9.00.

Chapter 12: 1920 - 1929 Flat Cards

Fold out valentine; anonymous publisher; printer markings: none; circa 1920s; no notice of copyright. $6.00 – 10.00.

Fold out valentine; anonymous publisher; printer markings: Made in Germany; circa 1920s – 1930s; no notice of copyright. $8.00 – 12.00.

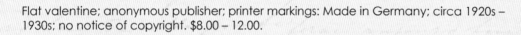

Flat valentine; anonymous publisher; printer markings: Made in Germany; circa 1920s – 1930s; no notice of copyright. $8.00 – 12.00.

Fold out valentine; anonymous publisher; printer markings: Made in Germany; circa 1920s – 1930s; no notice of copyright. $8.00 – 12.00.

Fold out tent shaped valentine; anonymous publisher; printer markings: Made in Germany; circa 1910s – 1920s; no notice of copyright. $8.00 – 12.00.

Flat valentine; anonymous publisher; printer markings: none; circa 1920s; no notice of copyright. $8.00 – 12.00.

Fold out valentine; anonymous publisher; printer markings: Made in Germany; circa 1910s – 1920s; no notice of copyright. $8.00 – 12.00.

1924

Flat valentine; anonymous publisher; printer markings: none; 1924; no notice of copyright. $8.00 – 13.00.

Flat valentine; anonymous publisher; printer markings: Printed in Germany; circa 1924; no notice of copyright. $6.00 – 9.00.

1925

Flat valentine; anonymous publisher; printer markings: none; 1925; no notice of copyright. $6.00 – 9.00.

Flat valentine; anonymous publisher; printer markings: Printed in Germany; circa 1925; no notice of copyright. $8.00 – 12.00.

Flat valentine; anonymous publisher; printer markings: Printed in Germany; circa 1920s; no notice of copyright. $8.00 – 12.00.

Fold out valentine; anonymous publisher; printer markings: none; circa 1920s; no notice of copyright. $6.00 – 9.00.

1926

Flat valentine; anonymous publisher; printer markings: none; 1926; no notice of copyright. $8.00 – 12.00.

Flat valentine; anonymous publisher; printer markings: none; 1926; no notice of copyright. $8.00 – 12.00.

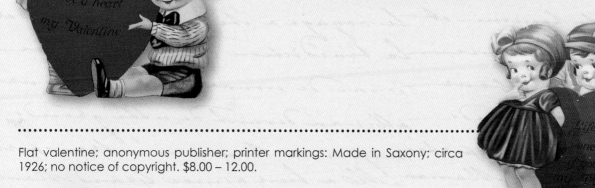

Flat valentine; anonymous publisher; printer markings: Made in Saxony; circa 1926 – 1927; no notice of copyright. $8.00 – 12.00.

Flat valentine; anonymous publisher; printer markings: Made in Saxony; circa 1926; no notice of copyright. $8.00 – 12.00.

Flat die-cut valentine; anonymous publisher; printer markings: Bavaria; circa 1926; no notice of copyright. $5.00 – 8.00.

Fold open valentine; anonymous publisher; printer markings: none; circa 1926; no notice of copyright. $5.00 – 8.00.

Flat die-cut valentine; anonymous publisher; printer markings: Bavaria; circa 1926; no notice of copyright. $5.00 – 8.00.

Flat die-cut valentine; anonymous publisher; printer markings: Bavaria; circa 1926; no notice of copyright. $5.00 – 8.00.

Flat die-cut valentine; anonymous publisher; printer markings: Bavaria; circa 1926; no notice of copyright. $5.00 – 8.00.

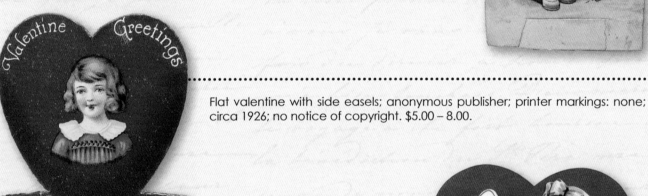

Flat die-cut valentine; anonymous publisher; printer markings: Bavaria; 1926; no notice of copyright. $5.00 – 8.00.

Flat valentine with side easels; anonymous publisher; printer markings: none; circa 1926; no notice of copyright. $5.00 – 8.00.

Flat valentine, 3-D effect; anonymous publisher; printer markings: none; circa 1910s – 1920s; no notice of copyright. $6.00 – 9.00.

Flat valentine with side easels; anonymous publisher; printer markings: none; circa 1926; no notice of copyright. $5.00 – 8.00.

Flat valentine; anonymous publisher; printer markings: none; circa 1920s; no notice of copyright. $8.00 – 12.00.

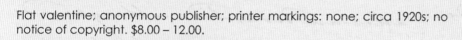

Fold out valentine; anonymous publisher; printer markings: none; circa 1920s; no notice of copyright. $8.00 – 12.00.

Flat valentine; anonymous publisher; printer markings: Germany; circa 1910s – 1920s; no notice of copyright. $8.00 – 12.00.

1927

Flat valentine; anonymous publisher; printer markings: Made in U.S.A.; 1927; no notice of copyright. $6.00 – 10.00.

Chapter 12: 1920 ~ 1929 Flat Cards

Giant fold out valentine; anonymous publisher; printer markings: none; circa 1920s – 1930s; no notice of copyright. $6.00 – 9.00.

Fold out valentine; anonymous publisher; printer markings: none; circa 1920s; no notice of copyright. $8.00 – 12.00.

Flat valentine with easel support; anonymous publisher; printer markings: none; circa 1920s; no notice of copyright. $6.00 – 10.00.

Fold out valentine; anonymous publisher; printer markings: none; circa 1920s – 1930s; no notice of copyright. $6.00 – 9.00.

Flat valentine with side easel supports; anonymous publisher; printer markings: none; circa 1920s – 1930s; no notice of copyright. $6.00 – 10.00.

Fold out valentine; anonymous publisher; printer markings: none; circa 1920s – 1930s; no notice of copyright. $6.00 – 9.00.

Flat valentine; anonymous publisher; printer markings: none; circa 1920s – 1930s; no notice of copyright. $6.00 – 9.00.

Fold out valentine; anonymous publisher; printer markings: none; circa 1920s – 1930s; no notice of copyright. $6.00 – 9.00.

Booklet valentine; anonymous publisher; printer markings: none; circa 1920s; no notice of copyright. $6.00 – 9.00.

Fold out valentine; anonymous publisher; printer markings: none; circa 1910s – 1930s; no notice of copyright. $6.00 – 9.00.

149

Fold out valentine; anonymous publisher; printer markings: none; circa 1920s – 1930s; no notice of copyright. $6.00 – 9.00.

Fold out valentine and lined envelope; anonymous publisher; printer markings: none; circa 1920s – 1930s; no notice of copyright. $6.00 – 9.00.

1928

Fold out valentine; anonymous publisher; printer markings: Germany and Made in Germany; circa 1928; no notice of copyright. $6.00 – 9.00.

Fold out valentine; anonymous publisher; printer markings: none; 1928; no notice of copyright. $6.00 – 9.00.

Fold out valentine; anonymous publisher; printer markings: Printed in Germany; circa 1928; no notice of copyright. $6.00 – 9.00.

Chapter 12: 1920 – 1929 *Flat Cards*

Fold out tent-shaped valentine; anonymous publisher; printer markings: none; 1928; no notice of copyright. $6.00 – 9.00.

Fold out tent-shaped valentine; anonymous publisher; printer markings: Made in Germany; circa 1928; no notice of copyright. $5.00 – 8.00.

Flat valentine; anonymous publisher; printer markings: Germany; 1928; no notice of copyright. $5.00 – 8.00.

Flat valentine; anonymous publisher; printer markings: Germany; 1928; no notice of copyright. $5.00 – 8.00.

Flat valentine; anonymous publisher; printer markings: Printed in Germany; circa 1920s; no notice of copyright. $5.00 – 8.00.

Flat valentine; anonymous publisher; printer markings: Germany; 1928; no notice of copyright. $5.00 – 8.00.

Fold out valentine; anonymous publisher; printer markings: Made in U.S.A.; 1928; no notice of copyright. $6.00 – 9.00.

Fold out valentine; anonymous publisher; printer markings: Made in U.S.A.; circa 1920s; no notice of copyright. $6.00 – 9.00.

Fold out valentine; anonymous publisher; printer markings: Made in U.S.A.; 1928; no notice of copyright. $6.00 – 9.00.

Flat valentine; anonymous publisher; printer markings: none; circa 1920s – 1930s; no notice of copyright. $6.00 – 9.00.

Flat valentine; anonymous publisher; printer markings: Germany; circa 1920s – 1930s; no notice of copyright. $5.00 – 8.00.

Flat valentine; anonymous publisher; printer markings: Printed in Germany; circa 1920s; no notice of copyright. $5.00 – 8.00.

Flat valentine; anonymous publisher; printer markings: Germany; circa 1920s; no notice of copyright. $5.00 – 8.00.

Flat valentine; anonymous publisher; printer markings: Made in Germany; circa 1920s – 1930s; no notice of copyright. $6.00 – 9.00.

Fold out valentine; anonymous publisher; printer markings: Germany; circa 1920s; no notice of copyright. $6.00 – 9.00.

Chapter 13
1920 ~ 1929
Fold Down Cards

The twenties saw a continuing interest in German-made fold down valentines. Even though the war had caused the cessation of German imports, Americans continued to admire and feel sentimental over exchanging fold down cards with chromolithograph scraps of delightful children and flowers. Fold down cards appear smaller in shape at times. They are difficult to distinguish from the previous decade except for the fact that a clever collector can see transitional changes in clothing, hairstyles, and modes of transportation that remain reference points in order to date the cards. Valentines retain the yearning for the sentimental by featuring cupids and flowers. They also indicate a shift in targeting a juvenile audience with subjects that appealed to children. Children undoubtedly maintained and perhaps even prolif-

erated the custom of giving out these valentines.

As Germany faced a decade of economic hardship after World War I and a period of hyperinflation, German cards could be made cheaply for export to America and elsewhere. Children and adults would enjoy many different new styles that retained certain elements of traditional cards a decade before. With the destruction of German factories and skilled workers in the Great War, machinery and manpower were lost. The fold down cards that resulted appear inferior in chromolithographic or engraved printing quality. They have a color depth with less range compared to the deeper, richer, and more varied colors of chromolithograph valentines of decades past. Nevertheless the lower quality printing did not seem to detract from the valentine's appeal to the sender or receiver.

Anonymously Published Card
Markings Indicating Place of Manufacture or Printing

- "Germany"
- "Made in Germany"
- "Printed in Bavaria"
- "Printed in Germany"

Types of Valentines Illustrated

- Fold down tent-shaped cards
- Fold downs in small sizes
- Fold downs in medium sizes
- Fold downs in miniature sizes
- Fold downs in large sizes
- Heart-shaped fold downs

Design Features Illustrated

- Chromolithograph scraps

Subjects Illustrated

- Airplanes
- Architecture with gables
- Architecture with turrets
- Birds
- Boats
- Bouquets of flowers

- Cars
- Child couples
- Children in old-fashioned dress
- Clover
- Cupids
- Daisies meaning in 1857: innocence[120]
- Doves
- Ducks
- Forget-me-not flowers meaning: true love[121]
- Fountains
- Google-eyed children
- Lighthouses
- Lily of the valley
- Musical instruments
- Musical instruments made from flowers
- Roses meaning in 1857: beauty[122]
- Shamrocks meaning: light heartedness[123]
- Sewing machines
- Ships
- Snowdrops
- Tennis rackets
- Trains

Exact years in captions are original sender/receiver dates.

Chapter 13: 1920 – 1929 Fold Down Cards

1921

Fold down valentine; anonymous publisher; printer markings: Made in Germany; 1921; no notice of copyright. $8.00 – 12.00.

Fold down valentine; anonymous publisher; printer markings: Printed in Germany; circa 1920s; no notice of copyright. $6.00 – 10.00.

Fold down valentine; anonymous publisher; printer markings: none; circa 1910s – 1920s; no notice of copyright. $6.00 – 10.00.

Fold down valentine; anonymous publisher; printer markings: none; circa 1920s; no notice of copyright. $10.00 – 18.00.

Miniature fold down valentine; anonymous publisher; printer markings: Printed in Germany; circa 1910s – 1920s; no notice of copyright. $6.00 – 10.00.

155

Miniature fold down valentine; anonymous publisher; printer markings: Printed in Germany; circa 1910s – 1920s; no notice of copyright. $6.00 – 10.00.

Miniature fold down valentine; anonymous publisher; printer markings: Printed in Germany; circa 1910s – 1920s; no notice of copyright. $6.00 – 10.00.

Miniature fold down valentine; anonymous publisher; printer markings: Made in Germany; circa 1910s – 1920s; no notice of copyright. $6.00 – 10.00.

Fold down valentine; anonymous publisher; printer markings: Made in Germany; circa 1920s – 1930s; no notice of copyright. $6.00 – 10.00.

Fold down valentine; anonymous publisher; printer markings: Printed in Germany; circa 1920s – 1930s; no notice of copyright. $6.00 – 10.00.

Fold down valentine; anonymous publisher; printer markings: Printed in Germany; circa 1920s – 1930s; no notice of copyright. $8.00 – 10.00.

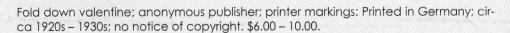

Fold down valentine; anonymous publisher; printer markings: Printed in Germany; circa 1920s – 1930s; no notice of copyright. $6.00 – 10.00.

Fold down valentine; anonymous publisher; printer markings: Printed in Germany; circa 1910s – 1920s; no notice of copyright. $8.00 – 10.00.

Fold down valentine; anonymous publisher; printer markings: Made in Germany; circa 1920s – early 1930s; no notice of copyright. $6.00 – 10.00.

Fold down valentine; anonymous publisher; printer markings: Printed in Germany; circa 1920s – early 1930s; no notice of copyright. $6.00 – 10.00.

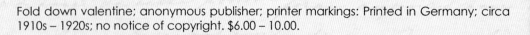

Fold down valentine; anonymous publisher; printer markings: Printed in Germany; circa 1920s – early 1930s; no notice of copyright. $6.00 – 10.00.

Fold down valentine; anonymous publisher; printer markings: Germany; circa 1920s – early 1930s; no notice of copyright. $6.00 – 10.00.

Fold down valentine; anonymous publisher; printer markings: Printed in Germany; circa 1910s – 1920s; no notice of copyright. $6.00 – 10.00.

Fold down valentine; anonymous publisher; printer markings: Printed in Germany; circa 1910s – 1920s; no notice of copyright. $6.00 – 10.00.

Fold down valentine; anonymous publisher; printer markings: Germany; circa 1920s – early 1930s; no notice of copyright. $6.00 – 10.00.

Fold down valentine; anonymous publisher; printer markings: Printed in Germany; circa 1910s – 1920s; no notice of copyright. $6.00 – 10.00.

Fold down valentine; anonymous publisher; printer markings: Printed in Germany; circa 1910s – 1920s; no notice of copyright. $6.00 – 10.00.

Fold down valentine; anonymous publisher; printer markings: Printed in Germany; circa 1910s – 1920s; no notice of copyright. $6.00 – 10.00.

Fold down valentine; anonymous publisher; printer markings: Printed in Germany; circa 1920s – 1930s; no notice of copyright. $6.00 – 10.00.

1924

Fold down valentine; anonymous publisher; printer markings: none; circa 1924; no notice of copyright. $6.00 – 10.00.

Fold down valentine; anonymous publisher; printer markings: Printed in Germany; 1924; no notice of copyright. $6.00 – 10.00.

1925

Fold down valentine; anonymous publisher; printer markings: Printed in Bavaria; circa 1925; no notice of copyright. $6.00 – 10.00.

Fold down valentine; anonymous publisher; printer markings: Germany; circa 1920s; no notice of copyright. $15.00 – 20.00.

Fold down valentine; anonymous publisher; printer markings: Printed in Germany; circa 1920s – 1930s; no notice of copyright. $6.00 – 10.00.

Fold down valentine; anonymous publisher; printer markings: Made in Germany; circa 1920s – 1930s; no notice of copyright. $6.00 – 10.00.

Fold down valentine; anonymous publisher; printer markings: Printed in Germany; circa 1920s – 1930s; no notice of copyright. $6.00 – 10.00.

Fold down valentine; anonymous publisher; printer markings: Germany; circa 1920s – 1930s; no notice of copyright. $10.00 – 15.00.

Fold down valentine; anonymous publisher; printer markings: Made in Germany; circa 1920s – 1930s; no notice of copyright. $10.00 – 15.00.

Fold down valentine; anonymous publisher; printer markings: Germany; circa 1920s – 1930s; no notice of copyright. $10.00 – 15.00.

Fold down valentine; anonymous publisher; printer markings: Printed in Bavaria; circa 1920s – 1930s; no notice of copyright. $8.00 – 12.00.

1926

Fold down valentine; anonymous publisher; printer markings: none; 1926; no notice of copyright. $6.00 – 10.00.

Fold down valentine; anonymous publisher; printer markings: Printed in Germany; circa 1920s – 1930s; no notice of copyright. $6.00 – 10.00.

Fold down valentine; anonymous publisher; printer markings: Printed in Germany; circa 1920s – 1930s; no notice of copyright. $6.00 – 10.00.

Fold down valentine; anonymous publisher; printer markings: Printed in Germany; circa 1920s – 1930s; no notice of copyright. $6.00 – 10.00.

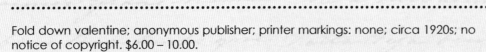

Fold down valentine; anonymous publisher; printer markings: none; circa 1920s; no notice of copyright. $6.00 – 10.00.

Chapter 13: 1920 ~ 1929 Fold Down Cards

Fold down valentine; anonymous publisher; printer markings: none; circa 1920s; no notice of copyright. $6.00 – 10.00.

Fold down valentine; anonymous publisher; printer markings: none; circa 1920s; no notice of copyright. $6.00 – 10.00.

Fold down valentine; anonymous publisher; printer markings: Printed in Germany; circa 1920s – 1930s; no notice of copyright. $6.00 – 10.00.

1927

Fold down valentine; anonymous publisher; printer markings: Printed in Germany; circa 1927; no notice of copyright. $10.00 – 15.00.

Fold down valentine; anonymous publisher; printer markings: Printed in Germany; 1927; no notice of copyright. $6.00 – 10.00.

Fold down valentine; anonymous publisher; printer markings: Printed in Germany; circa 1927; no notice of copyright. $10.00 – 15.00.

Fold down valentine; unknown publisher; printer markings: "G"; 1927; no notice of copyright. $10.00 – 15.00.

Fold down valentine; anonymous publisher; printer markings: Made in Germany; circa 1920s – 1930s; no notice of copyright. $6.00 – 10.00.

1928

Fold down valentine; anonymous publisher; printer markings: Printed in Germany; circa 1928; no notice of copyright. $10.00 – 15.00.

Fold down valentine; anonymous publisher; printer markings: Printed in Germany; circa 1928; no notice of copyright. $10.00 – 15.00.

Fold down valentine; anonymous publisher; printer markings: Made in Germany; circa 1920s – 1930s; no notice of copyright. $8.00 – 10.00.

Fold down valentine; anonymous publisher; printer markings: Made in Germany; circa 1920s – 1930s; no notice of copyright. $8.00 – 10.00.

Fold down valentine; anonymous publisher; printer markings: Made in Germany; circa 1920s – 1930s; no notice of copyright. $8.00 – 10.00.

Fold down valentine; anonymous publisher; printer markings: Made in Germany; circa 1910s – 1930s; no notice of copyright. $6.00 – 10.00.

Fold down valentine; anonymous publisher; printer markings: Germany; circa 1928; no notice of copyright. $10.00 – 15.00.

Fold down valentine; anonymous publisher; printer markings: Made in Germany; circa 1920s; no notice of copyright. $8.00 – 12.00.

Fold down valentine; anonymous publisher; printer markings: Made in Germany; circa 1920s; no notice of copyright. $8.00 – 12.00.

Fold down valentine; anonymous publisher; printer markings: Printed in Germany; circa 1920s – 1930s; no notice of copyright. $6.00 – 10.00.

Fold down valentine; anonymous publisher; printer markings: Made in Germany; circa 1920s; no notice of copyright. $6.00 – 10.00.

Fold down valentine; anonymous publisher; printer markings: Printed in Germany; circa 1920s; no notice of copyright. $6.00 – 10.00.

Fold down valentine; anonymous publisher; printer markings: Made in Germany; circa 1920s; no notice of copyright. $6.00 – 12.00.

Fold down valentine; anonymous publisher; printer markings: Germany; circa 1920s; no notice of copyright. $8.00 – 12.00.

Fold down valentine; anonymous publisher; printer markings: Germany; circa 1920s; no notice of copyright. $8.00 – 12.00.

Fold down valentine; anonymous publisher; printer markings: Made in Germany; circa 1920s; no notice of copyright. $8.00 – 12.00.

Fold down valentine; anonymous publisher; printer markings: none; circa 1920s; no notice of copyright. $8.00 – 12.00.

Fold down valentine; anonymous publisher; printer markings: Made in Germany; circa 1920s; no notice of copyright. $8.00 – 12.00.

1929

Fold down valentine; anonymous publisher; printer markings: Printed in Germany; 1929; no notice of copyright. $25.00 – 35.00.

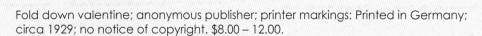

Fold down valentine; anonymous publisher; printer markings: Printed in Germany; circa 1929; no notice of copyright. $8.00 – 12.00.

Fold down valentine; anonymous publisher; printer markings: Printed in Germany; circa 1929; no notice of copyright. $6.00 – 10.00.

Fold down valentine; anonymous publisher; printer markings: Printed in Germany; circa 1929; no notice of copyright. $6.00 – 10.00.

Fold down valentine; anonymous publisher; printer markings: Printed in Germany; circa 1920s – 1930s; no notice of copyright. $6.00 – 10.00.

Fold down valentine; anonymous publisher; printer markings: Printed in Germany; circa 1910s – 1930s; no notice of copyright. $6.00 – 10.00.

Fold down valentine; anonymous publisher; printer markings: none; circa 1910s – 1930s; no notice of copyright. $6.00 – 10.00.

Fold down valentine; anonymous publisher; printer markings: Printed in Germany; circa 1910s – 1930s; no notice of copyright. $6.00 – 10.00.

Chapter 14
1920 - 1929
Mechanical Cards

Mechanical valentines with moveable subjects or features are novel and clever. Figures could tilt, appear to walk, bend, or perform various activities. Mechanical valentines had existed in the nineteenth century where arms, hats, and faces moved by pulling string or paper flaps.[124] Tastes for novel innovations in valentines changed over time as the public sought something fresh, modern, and catering to a juvenile audience. Mechanical valentines featuring juvenile themes had existed in the late teens. Quaint and childlike German mechanical valentines were very popular during the twenties. Examples have exaggerated personal features, caricatures, exotic animals, and figures moving to perform various activities. Besides animated subjects, mechanical valentines also included doors and windows that opened on houses featured on cards.

It is almost impossible to unravel the mystery of German mechanical valentines as one cannot ascertain certain key facts about them. The negative impacts of both World Wars decidedly resulted in the loss of skilled craftsmen, generations of printing expertise, specialized machinery, and written company records. Most valentines had no artist or manufacturer marks making it even more difficult to say for sure who designed or made the cards. Collectors never really know which cards were simply made by German manufacturers doing the print job for themselves for export sale or an American firm who sent their cards to be printed in Germany.

America's entry into World War I made it unfeasible for Americans to have traded with Germany or distasteful to sell any German-made goods. German-made or German printed valentines would not have been successfully sold in the United States during America's years at war. After the war Germany faced hard economic times. Economic difficulties began with the terms of the Treaty of Versailles, war reparations pay-

ments, and the eventual hyperinflation facing Germany in the twenties. German cards made and exported into the United States would have been inexpensive as a result of their circumstances since German workers would have been paid low wages. That allowed the Germans to keep exporting their valentines into America again after the war even though they now faced the competition from a developing American greeting card industry. German valentine artistry managed to survive the war's tribulations, weathered the distaste towards German goods, and survived again to offer their cards for American enjoyment.

These terrible setbacks make it almost impossible to historically trace with accuracy a full and clear picture of the origins of German valentines through these decades. Dating German cards can be very difficult as there is no notice or date of copyright by the printer or publisher. We must therefore rely on an original sender or receiver date as the greatest means of accurately dating them. Printer markings can sometimes hold clues. Markings on many German mechanicals that date them prior to the 1930s include "Printed in Germany" or "Germany." There do appear to be exceptions to this where some earlier than 1930 valentines read "Made in Germany," but for the most part the majority of "Made in Germany" cards appear to date from the 1930s by way of style. We can only speculate about the age of these cards and the possibilities of how the cards originated and ended their journeys into the United States. What is historically clear by their presence is that they flooded American shores during the 1920s. Their survival in abundance shows too they were most loved by their recipients and generations of collectors. German mechanicals have the most amazingly detailed color depth and imagination. These features made them attractive to contemporary children as well as the adults today that collect them.

Anonymously Published Card
Markings Indicating Place of Manufacture or Printing

- "Germany"

- "Printed in Germany"

Types of Valentines Illustrated

- Mechanical valentines — cards with moving parts

Design Features Illustrated

- Chromolithograph designs
- Mechanical arms
- Mechanical bodies
- Mechanical doors
- Mechanical legs
- Mechanical vehicles
- Metal chains
- Moving embellishments
- Moving eyes
- Paper fold out easel tabs

Subjects Illustrated

- Airplanes
- Alpine children
- Anthropomorphic hearts
- Boats
- Boys
- Cactus plants
- Cats
- Child couples
- Children with dogs
- Cottages
- Cupids
- Dogs
- Ducks
- Exotic animals
- Exotic birds
- Faces that change with multiple expressions
- Flower baskets
- Geese
- Girls
- Goats
- Gondolas
- Google-eyed children
- Hearts
- Hippos
- Horseback riding
- Motorcycles
- Moving umbrellas
- Musicians
- Period furniture
- Piano players
- Pigs
- Pirates
- Sailors
- Scooters
- Screen window blinds
- Seesaws
- Suitors
- Transportation
- Typists
- Umbrellas
- Walkers with moveable legs

Published Cards Not Illustrated

"C" or "E" Markings
Cards have a value of $8.00 – 16.00 each.
- 1920s mechanical, H.S. sailor boy, google-eye, mark on car, "C," possibly Carrington
- 1920s mechanical, girl crying, drying eyes, mark is "E," possibly Carrington

"C & E" and "H.B."
Cards have a value of $9.00 – 25.00 each.
- 1920s mechanical, google-eyed girl, "H.B."
- 1920s couple with umbrella folding out, "C & E"

Louis Katz
Artist cards have a value of $18.00 – 45.00 each.
- 1925 mechanical dog soldiers, "Attention Mark Time"
- 1928 mechanical valentine, fortune teller, Made in USA

Rectangle with "A.H." Marking
Artist mark "A.H." with rectangle. Cards have a value of $9.00 – 18.00 each.
- 1920s boy with stick fishing rod, yellow chick, bait can

Steicher Litho. Company, Rochester, New York
Cards have a value of $15.00 – 25.00 each.
- 1920s mechanical card, easel, girl holding valentine, purse, dog, and doll

Raphael Tuck
Cards have a value of $20.00 – 45.00 each.
- 1920s – 1930s mechanical, girl with moveable bonnet, easel, Printed in Saxony

Exact years in captions are original sender/receiver dates.

1922

Mechanical valentine, their eyes and her arm move; anonymous publisher; printer markings: none; 1922; no notice of copyright. $6.00 – 10.00.

Mechanical valentine booklet, eyes and hat move; anonymous publisher; printer markings: Made in U.S.A.; circa 1920s – 1930s; no notice of copyright. $8.00 – 15.00.

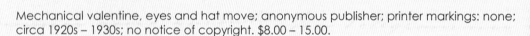

Mechanical valentine, eyes and hat move; anonymous publisher; printer markings: none; circa 1920s – 1930s; no notice of copyright. $8.00 – 15.00.

1923

Mechanical valentine with easel, birdcage moves; anonymous publisher; printer markings: none; circa 1910s – 1920s; no notice of copyright. $5.00 – 10.00.

Mechanical valentine, the dog's and girl's heads move; anonymous publisher; printer markings: Printed in Germany; 1923; no notice of copyright. $15.00 – 20.00.

Mechanical valentine with easel support, boy's upper body moves; anonymous publisher; printer markings: none; circa 1910s – 1920s ; no notice of copyright. $5.00 – 10.00.

Mechanical valentine with easel, boy moves; anonymous publisher; printer markings: Printed in Germany; circa 1920s – 1930s; no notice of copyright. $15.00 – 20.00.

Mechanical valentine, girl's upper body moves; anonymous publisher; printer markings: none; circa 1910s – 1920s; no notice of copyright. $5.00 – 10.00.

Mechanical valentine, boy's head and arms move; anonymous publisher; printer markings: Printed in Germany; circa 1924; no notice of copyright. $8.00 – 12.00.

1924

Mechanical valentine, girl's upper body moves; anonymous publisher; printer markings: Printed in Germany; circa 1924; no notice of copyright. $10.00 – 15.00.

Mechanical valentine, girl's facial expression changes with the turn of a wheel, view shows girl winking; anonymous publisher; printer markings: Made in Germany; circa 1920s – 1930s; no notice of copyright. $10.00 – 20.00.

View shows girl smiling.

View shows girl glancing to the side.

View shows girl crying.

Fold out valentine with moveable chain, dog stands out; anonymous publisher; printer markings: Made in Germany; circa 1920s – 1930s; no notice of copyright. $20.00 – 30.00.

Mechanical valentine, hippo's mouth moves; anonymous publisher; printer markings: Printed in Germany; circa 1924 – 1935; no notice of copyright. $15.00 – 20.00.

Mechanical valentine, goat's head and child's head in the tub move; anonymous publisher; printer markings: Printed in Germany; circa 1924 – 1935; no notice of copyright. $10.00 – 15.00.

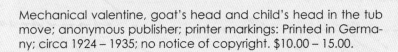

Mechanical valentine, pigs' legs and heads move; anonymous publisher; printer markings: Printed in Germany; circa 1924 – 1935; no notice of copyright. $15.00 – 20.00.

Mechanical valentine, cards, eyes, and head move; anonymous publisher; printer markings: Printed in Germany; circa 1924 – 1935; no notice of copyright. $12.00 – 18.00.

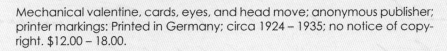

Mechanical valentine, lion's tongue and eyes move; anonymous publisher; printer markings: Made in U.S.A. No. 209-3; circa 1924 – 1935; no notice of copyright. $12.00 – 18.00.

1925

 *(see top-right card)*

Mechanical valentine, eyes and arm move; anonymous publisher; printer markings: Printed in Germany; 1925; no notice of copyright. $9.00 – 13.00.

Mechanical valentine with easel, carriage cover moves; anonymous publisher; printer markings: Printed in Germany; circa 1920s – 1930s; no notice of copyright. $9.00 – 13.00.

Mechanical valentine, boy's arm and wand move; anonymous publisher; printer markings: Germany; circa 1920s – 1930s; no notice of copyright. $12.00 – 18.00.

Mechanical valentine, watering can moves; anonymous publisher; printer markings: Printed in Germany; circa 1920s – 1930s; no notice of copyright. $9.00 – 13.00.

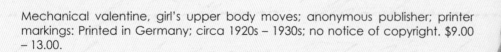

Mechanical valentine, girl's upper body moves; anonymous publisher; printer markings: Printed in Germany; circa 1920s – 1930s; no notice of copyright. $9.00 – 13.00.

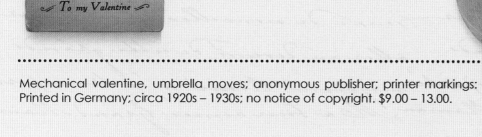

Mechanical valentine, boy's arm and accordion move; anonymous publisher; printer markings: Printed in Germany; circa 1920s – 1930s; no notice of copyright. $9.00 – 13.00.

Mechanical valentine, umbrella moves; anonymous publisher; printer markings: Printed in Germany; circa 1920s – 1930s; no notice of copyright. $9.00 – 13.00.

Mechanical valentine with easel, baby's and mother's arms move; anonymous publisher; printer markings: Printed in Germany; circa 1920s – 1930s; no notice of copyright. $9.00 – 13.00.

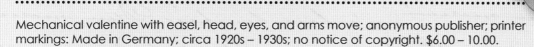

Mechanical valentine with easel, head, eyes, and arms move; anonymous publisher; printer markings: Made in Germany; circa 1920s – 1930s; no notice of copyright. $6.00 – 10.00.

Mechanical valentine with easel, head moves; anonymous publisher; printer markings: Germany; circa 1920s; no notice of copyright. $15.00 – 20.00.

Mechanical valentine, head moves; anonymous publisher; printer markings: Printed in Germany; circa 1920s – 1930s; no notice of copyright. $12.00 – 18.00.

Mechanical valentine with easel, dog and legs move; anonymous publisher; printer markings: none; circa 1920s; no notice of copyright. $15.00 – 20.00.

1928

Mechanical valentine, legs and mouth move; anonymous publisher; printer markings: Made in U.S.A.; 1928; no notice of copyright. $6.00 – 10.00.

Mechanical valentine, goose's neck grows and shrinks, feet move; anonymous publisher; printer markings: Printed in Germany; circa 1928; no notice of copyright. $25.00 – 35.00.

Chapter 14: 1920 – 1929 Mechanical Cards

Mechanical valentine with easel, upper body moves; anonymous publisher; printer markings: Made in Germany; 1928; no notice of copyright. $8.00 – 15.00.

Mechanical valentine with easel, upper body and goose move; anonymous publisher; printer markings: Germany; circa 1920s; no notice of copyright. $15.00 – 20.00.

Mechanical valentine, head and eyes move; anonymous publisher; printer markings: Made in Germany; 1928; no notice of copyright. $8.00 – 15.00.

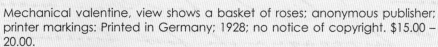

Mechanical valentine, view shows a basket of roses; anonymous publisher; printer markings: Printed in Germany; 1928; no notice of copyright. $15.00 – 20.00.

View shows girl jumping up from the basket of roses.

Mechanical valentine, view shows boy peeking over the left side of the bed; anonymous publisher; printer markings: Printed in Germany; circa 1928; no notice of copyright. $15.00 – 20.00.

View shows girl peeking over the right side of the bed.

Mechanical valentine; anonymous publisher; printer markings: none; circa 1920s; no notice of copyright. $15.00 – 20.00.

View shows a message of loving greetings when the tap is pulled up.

Fold out/stand-up valentine, eyes move; anonymous publisher; printer markings: none; circa 1920s; no notice of copyright. $25.00 – 35.00.

Fold out/stand-up valentine, eyes move; anonymous publisher; printer markings: Printed in Germany; circa 1920s; no notice of copyright. $25.00 – 35.00.

Mechanical valentine, eyes move; anonymous publisher; printer markings: Printed in Germany; circa 1920s; no notice of copyright. $10.00 – 20.00.

Mechanical valentine, eyes move; anonymous publisher; printer markings: none; circa 1920s; no notice of copyright. $10.00 – 20.00.

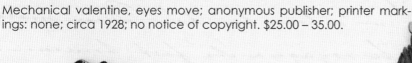

Mechanical valentine, eyes move; anonymous publisher; printer markings: none; circa 1928; no notice of copyright. $25.00 – 35.00.

Mechanical valentine, eyes move; anonymous publisher; printer markings: Made in U.S.A.; circa 1920s – 1930s; no notice of copyright. $5.00 – 8.00.

1929

Mechanical valentine, door opens; anonymous publisher; printer markings: Germany; 1929; no notice of copyright. $8.00 – 15.00.

Mechanical valentine with easel, dog's leg and head move; anonymous publisher; printer markings: Germany; 1929; no notice of copyright. $8.00 – 15.00.

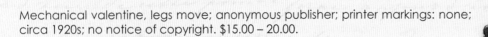

Mechanical valentine, legs move; anonymous publisher; printer markings: none; circa 1920s; no notice of copyright. $15.00 – 20.00.

Mechanical valentine, legs move; anonymous publisher; printer markings: none; circa 1920s; no notice of copyright. $15.00 – 20.00.

Mechanical valentine, wings move; anonymous publisher; printer markings: Germany; circa 1920s; no notice of copyright. $6.00 – 10.00.

Mechanical valentine, eyes move; anonymous publisher; printer markings: Printed in Germany; circa 1920s; no notice of copyright. $10.00 – 20.00.

Mechanical valentine, boat moves; anonymous publisher; printer markings: none; circa 1920s; no notice of copyright. $35.00 – 45.00.

Mechanical valentine, eyes move; anonymous publisher; printer markings: Printed in Germany; circa 1920s; no notice of copyright. $8.00 – 15.00.

Mechanical valentine, girl's upper body moves; anonymous publisher; printer markings: Printed in Germany; circa 1920s; no notice of copyright. $15.00 – 25.00.

Mechanical valentine with easel, head moves; anonymous publisher; printer markings: Made in Germany; circa 1920s – 1930s; no notice of copyright. $8.00 – 15.00.

Mechanical valentine with easel, head moves; anonymous publisher; printer markings: none; circa 1920s – 1930s; no notice of copyright. $8.00 – 12.00.

Mechanical valentine, eyes and mouth open; anonymous publisher; printer markings: none; circa 1920s; no notice of copyright. $30.00 – 45.00.

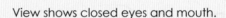

View shows closed eyes and mouth.

Mechanical valentine, window opens and closes; anonymous publisher; printer markings: Printed in Germany; circa 1920s; no notice of copyright. $12.00 – 18.00.

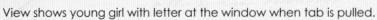

View shows young girl with letter at the window when tab is pulled.

Mechanical valentine with easel, door opens and closes; anonymous publisher; printer markings: Printed in Germany; circa 1920s – 1930s; no notice of copyright. $12.00 – 18.00.

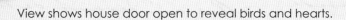

View shows house door open to reveal birds and hearts.

Mechanical valentine with easel, plane moves; anonymous publisher; printer markings: Made in Germany; circa 1920s – 1930s; no notice of copyright. $15.00 – 20.00.

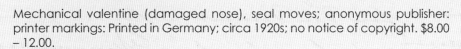

Mechanical valentine (damaged nose), seal moves; anonymous publisher; printer markings: Printed in Germany; circa 1920s; no notice of copyright. $8.00 – 12.00.

Mechanical valentine, umbrella moves; anonymous publisher; printer markings: Germany; circa 1920s – 1930s; no notice of copyright. $6.00 – 12.00.

Mechanical valentine, legs move; anonymous publisher; printer markings: Made in Germany; circa 1920s – 1930s; no notice of copyright. $8.00 – 15.00.

Mechanical valentine, donkey moves; anonymous publisher; printer markings: Printed in Germany; circa 1920s; no notice of copyright. $15.00 – 20.00.

Mechanical valentine, feet move; anonymous publisher; printer markings: Made in Germany; circa 1920s – 1930s; no notice of copyright. $8.00 – 15.00.

Mechanical valentine with easel, wheel moves; anonymous publisher; printer markings: Printed in Germany; circa 1920s; no notice of copyright. $10.00 – 15.00.

Mechanical valentine with easel, head and eyes move; anonymous publisher; printer markings: Printed in Germany; circa late 1920s; no notice of copyright. $10.00 – 15.00.

Mechanical valentine with easel, upper body moves; anonymous publisher; printer markings: Printed in Germany; circa 1920s; no notice of copyright. $15.00 – 25.00.

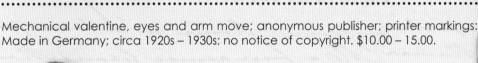

Mechanical valentine, eyes and arm move; anonymous publisher; printer markings: Made in Germany; circa 1920s – 1930s; no notice of copyright. $10.00 – 15.00.

Mechanical valentine, head moves; anonymous publisher; printer markings: Germany; circa 1910s – 1920s; no notice of copyright. $12.00 – 18.00.

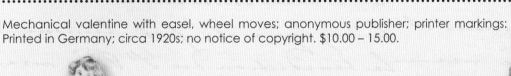

Mechanical valentine with easel, wheel moves; anonymous publisher; printer markings: Printed in Germany; circa 1920s; no notice of copyright. $10.00 – 15.00.

Mechanical valentine with easel, figure moves; anonymous publisher; printer markings: Printed in Germany; circa 1920s; no notice of copyright. $8.00 – 12.00.

Mechanical valentine with easel, eyes move; anonymous publisher; printer markings: none; circa late 1920s; no notice of copyright. $8.00 – 12.00.

Mechanical valentine with easel, figure moves; anonymous publisher; printer markings: Printed in Germany; circa 1920s; no notice of copyright. $8.00 – 12.00.

Mechanical valentine with easel, eyes move; anonymous publisher; printer markings: Printed in Germany; 1929; no notice of copyright. $8.00 – 12.00.

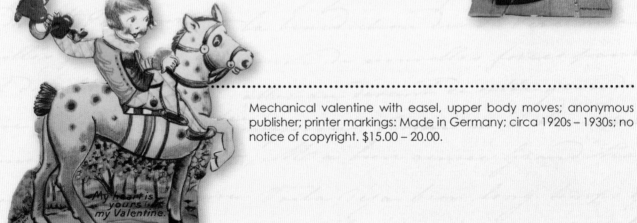

Mechanical valentine with easel, upper body moves; anonymous publisher; printer markings: Made in Germany; circa 1920s – 1930s; no notice of copyright. $15.00 – 20.00.

Mechanical valentine, upper bodies move; anonymous publisher; printer markings: Germany; circa 1920s; no notice of copyright. $15.00 – 25.00.

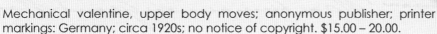

Mechanical valentine, upper body moves; anonymous publisher; printer markings: Germany; circa 1920s; no notice of copyright. $15.00 – 20.00.

Mechanical valentine, upper body and laundry moves; anonymous publisher; printer markings: Printed in Germany; circa 1920s; no notice of copyright. $12.00 – 18.00.

Mechanical valentine with easel, eyes move; anonymous publisher; printer markings: Made in Germany; circa 1920s – 1930s; no notice of copyright. $6.00 – 12.00.

Mechanical valentine, stop sign moves; anonymous publisher; printer markings: Printed in Germany; circa 1920s; no notice of copyright. $25.00 – 35.00.

Mechanical valentine, seesaw moves; anonymous publisher; printer markings: Germany; circa 1920s; no notice of copyright. $25.00 – 35.00.

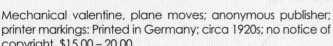

Mechanical valentine, plane moves; anonymous publisher; printer markings: Printed in Germany; circa 1920s; no notice of copyright. $15.00 – 20.00.

Mechanical valentine, head moves; anonymous publisher; printer markings: Made in Germany; circa 1920s – 1930s; no notice of copyright. $15.00 – 20.00.

Mechanical valentine, eyes and cupid move; anonymous publisher; printer markings: Made in Germany; circa 1920s – 1930s; no notice of copyright. $8.00 – 12.00.

Mechanical valentine, cupid and letters move; anonymous publisher; printer markings: Made in Germany; circa 1920s – 1930s; no notice of copyright. $10.00 – 18.00.

Mechanical valentine with easel, girl ascends and descends; anonymous publisher; printer markings: Made in Germany; circa 1920s – 1930s; no notice of copyright. $10.00 – 15.00.

Mechanical valentine with easel, upper body and arm move; anonymous publisher; printer markings: Made in Germany; circa 1920s – 1930s; no notice of copyright. $12.00 – 18.00.

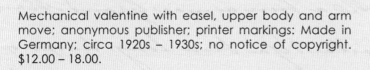

191

Chapter 15
1860s ~ 1920s
Novelty Cards

Novelty valentines are the most unusual and imaginative forms of valentines. They might be a chromolithograph fan showing beautiful children, hearts, or flowers. A novelty valentine could be of the hanging variety with several pieces of chromolithography separated by ribbon or string. Others might be meant to hang on a wall or displayed with the card's own easel with stiff parchment paper incorporated into the design. Rare novelty cards existed in the nineteenth century. Most prevalent novelty valentines date to the first two decades of the twentieth century. Still eager for the unusual, valentine makers of the 1920s and 1930s created their own beautiful version of valentine fans. Collectors can admire every novel example's innovation as an important addition to their collection.

Important Valentine Manufacturers, Publishers, and Printers

- Ernest Nister
- Raphael Tuck

Types of Valentines Illustrated

- Hanging valentines
- Lollipop cards
- Stiff cardboard and parchment easel valentines
- Valentine fans
- Wall hanging valentines

Design Features Illustrated

- Chromolithography
- Ribbons
- String and silk tassels

Subjects Illustrated

- Art Nouveau scrolls and flourishes
- Birds
- Butterflies
- Cats
- Children
- Cupid postmen
- Cupids
- Flowers
- Hearts
- Lilies meaning in 1857: purity and modesty[125]
- Pansies meaning: thoughts[126]
- Roses meaning in 1857: beauty[127]
- Scenes of outdoors
- Stiff parchment ornamentation
- Windmills

Published Cards Not Illustrated

E. Rosen Company, Providence, Rhode Island, Lollipop Holder Cards
Cards have a value of $5.00 – 15.00 each.
- 1938 man with hat wearing checkered overalls and polka dot shirt, "Ay tank ay go..."
- 1930s – 1940s boy with cannon, "Pop, pop..." inscription
- 1930s – 1940s cowboy with lasso
- 1930s – 1940s girl with bag, "I'm a poor country cousin...," red and white colored card
- 1930s – 1940s two dogs, "Puppy love is dandy," red and white card
- 1930s – 1940s woman on wagon, "Please take my heart"
- 1930s – 1940s Humpty Dumpty on a wall, red and white colored card
- 1930s girl reading book on heart printed wing chair, "Please put up your book," red and white card
- 1940s boy and girl couple with sun and hearts
- 1940s boy in military jacket, newspaper, sailor hat with wheelbarrow filled with lollipops
- 1940s boy serenading girl with heart-shaped instrument
- 1940s drummer boy, multicolored card
- 1940s farmer boy with hoe and heart plant
- 1940s girl and boy on tricycle, "Honey you're the top," orange, yellow, and black card

Exact years in captions are original sender/receiver dates.

Hanging valentine with ribbon, applied scrap, and stiff cardboard backing; anonymous publisher; printer markings: none; circa late 1900s – early 1910s; no notice of copyright. $10.00 – 15.00.

Hanging valentine with ribbon, applied scrap, and stiff cardboard backing; anonymous publisher; printer markings: none; circa late 1900s – early 1910s; no notice of copyright. $10.00 – 15.00.

Hanging valentine with ribbon, applied scrap, and stiff cardboard backing; unknown publisher; printer markings: "G"; circa late 1900s – early 1910s; no notice of copyright. $10.00 – 15.00.

Rare chromolithograph mechanical fan out valentine, floral leaves move when thread linking them is pulled; publisher: none; printer markings: none; late 1860s; no notice of copyright. $100.00 – 200.00.

3-D effect hanging valentine, small cupid dangles hang from silk ribbons; anonymous publisher; printer markings: none; 1900s – 1910s; no notice of copyright. $45.00 – 85.00.

Easel card with stiffened parchment paper, applied lace, and scrap; anonymous publisher; printer markings: none; circa 1890s – 1900s; no notice of copyright. $25.00 – 45.00.

Rare mechanical card of an unhappy flower with moveable face; publisher: Ernest Nister; printer markings: Ernest Nister, London, New York, E.P. Dutton & Co., Printed in Bavaria, No 3250; circa 1890s – 1910s; no notice of copyright. $100.00 – 250.00.

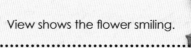

View shows the flower smiling.

Fold open valentine with applied scrap front and second scene inside, ribbon embellishment; anonymous publisher; printer markings: none; circa 1910s; no notice of copyright. $10.00 – 15.00.

Hanging valentine with applied parchment; anonymous publisher; printer markings: none; circa 1900s; no notice of copyright. $25.00 – 45.00.

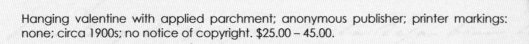

Part of a hanging valentine; anonymous publisher; printer markings: none; circa 1900s; no notice of copyright. $8.00 – 15.00.

Hanging valentine with applied parchment; anonymous publisher; printer markings: none; circa 1900s; no notice of copyright. $25.00 – 45.00.

Part of a hanging valentine; anonymous publisher; printer markings: none; circa 1900s; no notice of copyright. $8.00 – 15.00.

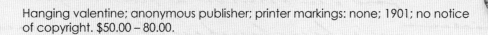

Hanging valentine; anonymous publisher; printer markings: none; 1901; no notice of copyright. $50.00 – 80.00.

Part of a hanging valentine; anonymous publisher; printer markings: none; circa 1900s; no notice of copyright. $8.00 – 15.00.

Chapter 15: 1860s – 1920s Novelty Cards

Hanging valentine; anonymous publisher; printer markings: none; circa 1900s; no notice of copyright. $30.00 – 40.00.

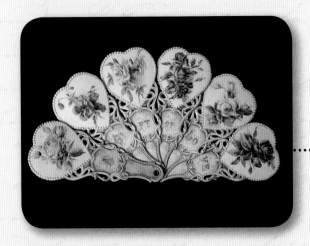

Valentine fan, "A Gift of Love"; anonymous publisher; printer markings: none; 1901; no notice of copyright. $100.00 – 300.00.

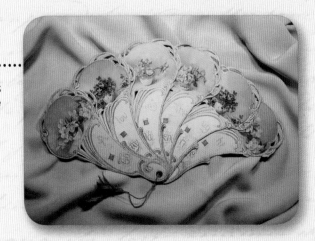

Valentine fan, "A Loving Thought to My Valentine"; anonymous publisher; printer markings: none; circa 1890s – 1900s; no notice of copyright. $100.00 – 300.00.

Hanging valentine; anonymous publisher; printer markings: none; circa 1900s – 1910s; no notice of copyright. $35.00 – 55.00.

Valentine fan, "A Greeting From Thy Valentine With Kindest Regards"; anonymous publisher; printer markings: none; circa 1900s – 1910s; no notice of copyright. $100.00 – 300.00.

Hanging valentine; publisher: Ernest Nister in London and E.P. Dutton & Co., in New York; printer markings: Printed in Bavaria 117; circa 1900s; no notice of copyright. $45.00 – 75.00.

Hanging valentine; anonymous publisher; printer markings: none; 1909; no notice of copyright. $25.00 – 55.00.

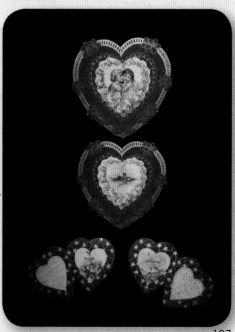

Hanging valentine (missing ribbons or strings); anonymous publisher; printer markings: none; circa 1900s – 1910s; no notice of copyright. $35.00 – 55.00.

Valentine fan; anonymous publisher; printer markings: Germany; circa mid 1920s; no notice of copyright. $35.00 – 65.00.

Valentine fan; anonymous publisher; printer markings: none; circa mid 1920s; no notice of copyright. $35.00 – 65.00.

Folded valentine fan; anonymous publisher; printer markings: none; circa 1920s – early 1930s; no notice of copyright. $20.00 – 40.00.

Open view of valentine fan.

Chapter 16
1900s - 1930s
Stand-Up Valentines

Stand-up valentines are the most grandiose show-stoppers with the most details, layers, chromolithograph scraps, and accents. Dating from the 1890s through the 1930s these special valentines represent the most magnificent examples of their decades. Using multilayered design features, these fold out cards are the crowning touch to a collection. Many of these cards were anonymously published and printed. Many originated in Germany showing the chromolithographer's art at its finest.

Dating the cards can be difficult and collectors may have to depend on the hand dating of the sender or receiver. Their lack of copyright and publisher information can only add to their mystery and timeless appeal. Clues to dating the cards lie in their rich colors, subject clothing, transportation styles, and contemporary children's hairstyles. They should be dated conservatively as there is no documentation on anonymous cards to prove or disprove if one design was used for more than one year.

Important Valentine Manufacturers, Publishers, and Printers

- Gibson Art Company

Anonymously Published Card
Markings Indicating Place of Manufacture or Printing

- "Germany"
- "Printed in Germany"

Types of Valentines Illustrated

- Large fold down valentines
- Large fold out valentines
- Large stand-up valentines
- Stand-up and fold out valentines

Design Features Illustrated

- German-made chromolithograph scraps
- Glossy paper quality
- Heavy paper stock

Subjects Illustrated

- Arches
- Boats
- Bouquets
- Bridges
- Cannons
- Cars
- Carriages
- Chariots
- Children
- Classical columns
- Cupids
- Doves
- Forget-me-nots meaning: true love[128]
- Garden arches
- Garden fences
- Gates
- Hearts
- Ladies
- Lilacs meaning in 1857: first emotions of love[129]
- Lily of the valley meaning in 1857: return of happiness[130]
- Roses meaning in 1857: beauty[131]
- Ships
- Swallows
- Urns
- Wheelbarrows filled with flowers

Exact years in captions are original sender/receiver dates.

Large stand-up valentine (damaged head); anonymous publisher; printer markings: Germany; circa 1900s – 1910s; no notice of copyright. $75.00 – 175.00.

Stand-up and fold out valentine; anonymous publisher; printer markings: none; circa 1900s; no notice of copyright. $55.00 – 75.00.

Large fold out valentine; anonymous publisher; printer markings: Printed in Germany; circa 1900s; no notice of copyright. $100.00 – 300.00.

Large stand-up valentine; anonymous publisher; printer markings: none; circa 1900s; no notice of copyright. $45.00 – 65.00.

Stand-up die-cut with fold out flower; publisher: Gibson Art Company; printer markings: "G" inside artist easel trademark, Printed in Germany; circa 1910s; no notice of copyright. $40.00 – 65.00.

Large fold out valentine; anonymous publisher; printer markings: Printed in Germany; circa 1900s; no notice of copyright. $75.00 – 200.00.

Stand-up die-cut with fold out flower; publisher: Gibson Art Company; printer markings: "G" inside artist easel trademark, Printed in Germany; circa 1910s; no notice of copyright. $40.00 – 65.00.

Large stand-up valentine; anonymous publisher; printer markings: none; circa 1910s – 1920s; no notice of copyright. $75.00 – 150.00.

Fold out valentine; anonymous publisher; printer markings: none; circa 1920s; no notice of copyright. $75.00 – 150.00.

Large fold out valentine; anonymous publisher; printer markings: none; circa 1910s – 1920s; no notice of copyright. $55.00 – 130.00.

Large stand-up valentine; anonymous publisher; printer markings: Printed in Germany; circa 1910s; no notice of copyright. $200.00 – 300.00.

Large stand-up valentine; anonymous publisher; printer markings: Printed in Germany; circa 1900s – 1910s; no notice of copyright. $200.00 – 300.00.

Large stand-up valentine; anonymous publisher; printer markings: none; circa 1900s – 1910s; no notice of copyright. $200.00 – 300.00.

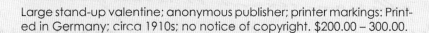

Large stand-up valentine; anonymous publisher; printer markings: Printed in Germany; circa 1910s; no notice of copyright. $200.00 – 300.00.

1924

Large stand-up valentine; anonymous publisher; printer markings: Printed in Germany; circa 1924; no notice of copyright. $70.00 – 145.00.

1925

Large stand-up valentine; anonymous publisher; printer markings: Printed in Germany; circa 1925; no notice of copyright. $70.00 – 145.00.

Large stand-up valentine; anonymous publisher; printer markings: Printed in Germany; circa 1920s; no notice of copyright. $100.00 – 200.00.

1927

Large stand-up valentine; anonymous publisher; printer markings: Printed in Germany; 1927; no notice of copyright. $200.00 – 300.00.

1928

Large stand-up valentine; anonymous publisher; printer markings: none; circa 1928; no notice of copyright. $75.00 – 150.00.

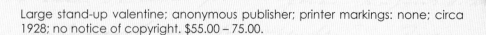

Large stand-up valentine; anonymous publisher; printer markings: none; circa 1928; no notice of copyright. $55.00 – 75.00.

1929

Large stand-up valentine; anonymous publisher; printer markings: Printed in Germany and "G"; 1929; no notice of copyright. $55.00 – 75.00.

Large fold out valentine; anonymous publisher; printer markings: none; circa 1920s; no notice of copyright. $200.00 – 300.00.

Chapter 17
1930 - 1939
Flat Cards

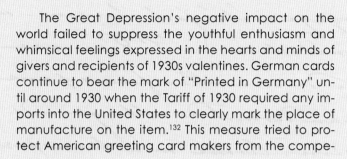

The Great Depression's negative impact on the world failed to suppress the youthful enthusiasm and whimsical feelings expressed in the hearts and minds of givers and recipients of 1930s valentines. German cards continue to bear the mark of "Printed in Germany" until around 1930 when the Tariff of 1930 required any imports into the United States to clearly mark the place of manufacture on the item.[132] This measure tried to protect American greeting card makers from the competition of foreign imports that were cheaply made. The abundance of cards labeled before and after this time bear different inscriptions while the "Made in Germany" stamp appears to be prevalent after 1930, there are still some cards that bear that marking before 1930 and some that bear the mark "Printed in Germany" after 1930. Collectors of domestic cards note their 1930s valentines were marked "Made in U.S.A." but many indicate no manufacturer.

Types of Valentines Illustrated

- Die-cuts
- Flat valentines
- Fold open valentines
- Rebus cards

Design Features Illustrated

- Glossy paper
- Gold printing on paper
- Thin quality paper

Subjects Illustrated

- Art Deco styled borders
- Beach themes
- Boats
- Boys
- Cars
- Cats
- Children
- Clowns
- Comic book style characters
- Common objects
- Dogs
- Ducks
- Elephants
- Flowers with girl's heads
- Food
- Girls
- Lawn mowers
- Magicians
- Musicians
- Nursery rhyme characters
- Old-fashioned girls
- Planes
- School desks
- Stained glass effect borders
- Telephones
- Tennis
- Tricycles
- Umbrellas
- Vegetables with girls
- Wagons

Published Cards Not Illustrated

A.C. Co., Product of U.S.A.
Cards have a value of $6.00 – 9.00 each.
- 1930s – 1940s boy and girl at grocery store
- 1930s boy and girl on swing
- 1936 – 1940s policeman
- 1936 – 1940s postman, special delivery

American Colortype Co.
Trademark: American Colortype, Torch Radiating
Cards have a value of $6.00 – 9.00 each.
- 1930s early Art Deco style boy and girl sitting on a fence
- 1930s man breaking through large heart, girl and dog

Americard
Cards have a value of $6.00 – 12.00 each.
- 1930s bears with white lace overlay
- 1930s boy and girl at a market store shopping, "A Heart for Sale"
- 1930s boy in boat fishing
- 1930s boy with girl in jail
- 1930s boy with puppy, lace
- 1930s clown boy
- 1930s fold out boy boxing
- 1930s fold out couple

Chapter 17: 1930 – 1939 Flat Cards

- 1930s fold out girl with fold out purse
- 1930s heart and lace, dog
- 1930s "Let's strike a match," book of matches
- 1930s pocket knife, "You're plenty sharp."
- 1930s policeman and girl in muff outfit, fold out
- 1930s puppy and kitten in wagon
- 1939 "Dear Teacher" card, heart and bell
- 1930s – 1940s boy blowing bubbles, Made in USA
- 1930s – 1940s clowning around
- 1930s – 1940s farmer boy pitching hay, Made in USA
- 1930s – 1940s mechanical girl with cake
- 1930s – 1940s boy with tire filling with air

Charles Twelvetrees, "CT" artist signature
Cards have a value of $8.00 – 12.00 each.
- 1930s duck baby pop-up, CT artist signature
- 1930s girl in car, CT artist signature

Carrington
Cards have a value of $6.00 – 15.00 each.
Trademarks: tree outline with E, H, or A inside.
- 1930s boy on sleigh
- 1930s boy sitting on bench chair
- 1930s boy ties girl to a tree with garland
- 1930s boy with accordion
- 1930s boy with snowball
- 1930s child couple
- 1930s children
- 1930s children and dog, google eyes
- 1930s children, heart-shaped card
- 1930s couple
- 1930s couple under umbrella
- 1930s girl in green kimono jacket, yellow background, heart-shaped die-cut
- 1930s girl on beach
- 1930s girl with ballot
- 1930s girl with doll
- 1930s girl with Scottie dog and dog house
- 1930s goat with man
- 1930s mechanical valentine, children with ice cream
- 1930s old-fashioned couple
- 1930s old-fashioned girl at a mailbox, fold down card
- 1930s sailor boy
- 1930s sailor girl
- 1930s two African American children, fold down card
- 1939 boy, "Ok toots I am yours"
- 1930s – 1940s boy with jack card

C. Co., Made in USA
Cards have a value of $6.00 – 15.00 each.
- 1930s girl in bonnet
- 1930s – 1940s two children, ice cream cone

Designed by Davis Company
Cards have a value of $6.00 – 9.00 each.
- 1934 girl with wooden spoon

Diamond Valentines (H in diamond logo), Made in USA
Cards have a value of $6.00 – 9.00 each.
- 1930s boy in yellow skirt, girl in red dress, floral heart and lace overlay

Disney, Walt Disney Productions
Cards have a value of $20.00 – 40.00 each.
- Pinocchio's Clio the fish, Copyright 1939, W.D.P. Made in U.S.A.
- Pinocchio's Puppet Show, Copyright 1939, W.D.P. Made in U.S.A.

Double Glo
Cards have a value of $9.00 – 12.00 each.
- 1930s blonde girl angel with heart, lace overlay, Made in USA
- 1930s girl in ocean swimming, Made in USA

The Fairfield Line, Made in USA
Cards have a value of $6.00 – 9.00 each.
- 1930s swans on lake, square scalloped card

Gibson Cincinnati, U.S.A.
Cards have a value of $6.00 – 9.00 each.
- 1930s cat with bouquet
- 1930s couple on bench
- 1930s girl in boat with hearts
- 1930s girl raking hearts
- 1930s puppies with basket of hearts
- 1939 girl in pink chair with blue book

Hallmark
Cards have a value of $15.00 – 40.00 each.
- 1930s mechanical wheels, red car, couples, "A Hallmark Card"
- 1939 valentine with buds and pig in the tub

International Art, eagle on globe logo
Cards have a value of $6.00 – 12.00 each.
- 1930s girl and boy on fence

Whitney Made
Cards have a value of $8.00 – 24.00 each.
- 1930 boy in blue and white suit, girl in pink dress, rose border, small rectangular card
- 1930 girl and boy skating, pink roses, small rectangular card
- 1930 girl in green dress, blonde hair, holding a doll looking over her left shoulder, small rectangular card
- 1930 girl on swing, orange dress, pink colors too, small rectangular card
- 1931 black haired girl in green dress, floral border, heart-shaped card
- 1930s lace valentine with girl sipping soda from a cup using a straw, ivory lace over print

Exact years in captions are original sender/receiver dates.

Chapter 17: 1930 – 1939 *Flat Cards*

1930

Fold open valentine; anonymous publisher; printer markings: none; 1930; no notice of copyright. $5.00 – 7.00.

Fold open valentine; anonymous publisher; printer markings: none; 1930; no notice of copyright. $6.00 – 9.00.

Fold open valentine; anonymous publisher; printer markings: none; circa 1920s – 1930s; no notice of copyright. $6.00 – 9.00.

Fold open valentine, back (left) and front (right); anonymous publisher; printer markings: none; 1930; no notice of copyright. $6.00 – 9.00.

Fold open valentine, back (left) and front (right); anonymous publisher; printer markings: none; circa 1920s – 1930s; no notice of copyright. $6.00 – 9.00.

Fold open valentine; anonymous publisher; printer markings: none; circa 1920s – 1930s; no notice of copyright. $6.00 – 9.00.

Fold open valentine, front view of a little boy in a sailor suit; anonymous publisher; printer markings: none; circa 1930s; no notice of copyright. $6.00 – 9.00.

Back view of the card showing a little girl holding a valentine.

Fold open valentine; anonymous publisher; printer markings: none; circa 1920s – 1930s; no notice of copyright. $6.00 – 9.00.

Fold open valentine; anonymous publisher; printer markings: none; circa 1920s – 1930s; no notice of copyright. $6.00 – 9.00.

Fold open valentine; anonymous publisher; printer markings: Made in Germany; circa 1920s – 1930s; no notice of copyright. $6.00 – 9.00.

Fold open valentine; anonymous publisher; printer markings: none; circa 1930s; no notice of copyright. $6.00 – 9.00.

Fold open valentine; anonymous publisher; printer markings: none; circa 1920s – 1930s; no notice of copyright. $6.00 – 9.00.

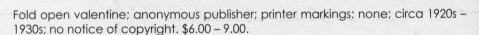

Fold open valentine; anonymous publisher; printer markings: none; circa 1920s – 1930s; no notice of copyright. $6.00 – 9.00.

Fold open valentine; anonymous publisher; printer markings: Made in U.S.A.; circa 1930s; no notice of copyright. $6.00 – 9.00.

Chapter 17: 1930 – 1939 *Flat Cards*

Fold open valentine; anonymous publisher; printer markings: Made in U.S.A.; circa 1930s; no notice of copyright. $6.00 – 9.00.

Fold open valentine; anonymous publisher; printer markings: none; circa 1920s – 1930s; no notice of copyright. $6.00 – 9.00.

Fold open valentine; anonymous publisher; printer markings: Printed in U.S.A.; circa 1920s – 1930s; no notice of copyright. $6.00 – 9.00.

1931

Flat valentine; anonymous publisher; printer markings: Made in U.S.A.; 1931; no notice of copyright. $6.00 – 9.00.

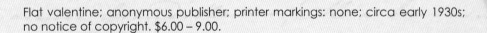

Flat valentine; anonymous publisher; printer markings: none; circa early 1930s; no notice of copyright. $6.00 – 9.00.

Flat valentine; anonymous publisher; printer markings: Made in U.S.A.; circa early 1930s; no notice of copyright. $6.00 – 9.00.

Fold open valentine; anonymous publisher; printer markings: Printed in Germany; circa 1931; no notice of copyright. $9.00 – 18.00.

Flat valentine; anonymous publisher; printer markings: Printed in Germany; 1931; no notice of copyright. $9.00 – 18.00.

Fold open valentine; anonymous publisher; printer markings: Printed in Germany; 1931; no notice of copyright. $9.00 – 18.00.

Flat valentine; anonymous publisher; printer markings: Made in U.S.A.; 1931; no notice of copyright. $6.00 – 9.00.

Fold open valentine; anonymous publisher; printer markings: Made in U.S.A.; 1931; no notice of copyright. $6.00 – 9.00.

Flat valentine; anonymous publisher; printer markings: Made in U.S.A.; 1931; no notice of copyright. $6.00 – 9.00.

Booklet valentine; anonymous publisher; printer markings: Made in U.S.A.; circa 1930s; no notice of copyright. $8.00 – 10.00.

Flat valentine; anonymous publisher; printer markings: Made in U.S.A.; circa 1930s; no notice of copyright. $6.00 – 9.00.

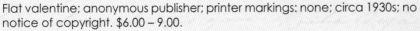

Flat valentine; anonymous publisher; printer markings: none; circa 1930s; no notice of copyright. $6.00 – 9.00.

Fold open valentine; anonymous publisher; printer markings: none; 1931; no notice of copyright. $8.00 – 10.00.

Fold open valentine; anonymous publisher; printer markings: none; circa 1931; no notice of copyright. $8.00 – 10.00.

Fold open valentine; anonymous publisher; printer markings: none; 1931; no notice of copyright. $8.00 – 10.00.

Fold open valentine; anonymous publisher; printer markings: none; circa late 1920s – early 1930s; no notice of copyright. $8.00 – 10.00.

Flat valentine; anonymous publisher; printer markings: Germany; circa 1920s – 1930s; no notice of copyright. $6.00 – 9.00.

Fold open valentine; anonymous publisher; printer markings: none; circa late 1920s – early 1930s; no notice of copyright. $8.00 –10.00.

1932

Fold open valentine; anonymous publisher; printer markings: Made in U.S.A.; 1932; no notice of copyright. $6.00 – 9.00.

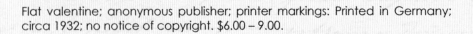

Flat valentine; anonymous publisher; printer markings: Printed in Germany; circa 1932; no notice of copyright. $6.00 – 9.00.

Fold open valentine; anonymous publisher; printer markings: none; 1931 – 1932; no notice of copyright. $6.00 – 9.00.

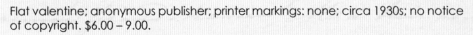

Flat valentine; anonymous publisher; printer markings: none; circa 1930s; no notice of copyright. $6.00 – 9.00.

Chapter 17: 1930 – 1939 Flat Cards

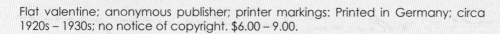

Flat valentine; anonymous publisher; printer markings: none; circa 1930s; no notice of copyright. $6.00 – 9.00.

Flat valentine; anonymous publisher; printer markings: Printed in Germany; circa 1920s – 1930s; no notice of copyright. $6.00 – 9.00.

1933

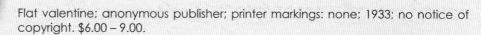

Flat valentine; anonymous publisher; printer markings: none; 1933; no notice of copyright. $6.00 – 9.00.

Flat valentine; anonymous publisher; printer markings: none; circa 1933; no notice of copyright. $6.00 – 9.00.

Flat valentine; anonymous publisher; printer markings: Made in U.S.A.; circa 1930s; no notice of copyright. $6.00 – 9.00.

Fold open valentine; anonymous publisher; printer markings: none; circa 1930s; no notice of copyright. $6.00 – 9.00.

Fold open valentine; anonymous publisher; printer markings: none; circa 1930s; no notice of copyright. $6.00 – 9.00.

1934

Flat valentine with side fold out easels; anonymous publisher; printer markings: Made in Germany; circa 1934; no notice of copyright. $6.00 – 9.00.

Flat valentine with side fold out easels; anonymous publisher; printer markings: Made in Germany; 1934; no notice of copyright. $6.00 – 9.00.

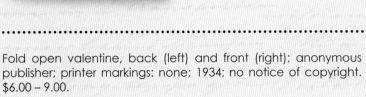

Fold open valentine, back (left) and front (right); anonymous publisher; printer markings: none; 1934; no notice of copyright. $6.00 – 9.00.

Fold open valentine, back (left) and front (right); anonymous publisher; printer markings: none; 1934; no notice of copyright. $6.00 – 9.00.

Fold open valentine, back (left) and front (right); anonymous publisher; printer markings: none; circa 1920s – 1930s; no notice of copyright. $6.00 – 9.00.

Flat valentine; anonymous publisher; printer markings: Printed in Germany; circa 1934; no notice of copyright. $8.00 – 12.00.

Flat valentine; anonymous publisher; printer markings: Printed in Germany; circa 1934; no notice of copyright. $8.00 – 12.00.

Flat valentine; anonymous publisher; printer markings: Printed in Germany; circa 1934; no notice of copyright. $8.00 – 12.00.

Chapter 17: 1930 ~ 1939 *Flat Cards*

Flat valentine; anonymous publisher; printer markings: Printed in Germany; circa 1934; no notice of copyright. $8.00 – 12.00.

Flat valentine; anonymous publisher; printer markings: Germany; circa 1934; no notice of copyright. $8.00 – 12.00.

Flat valentine; anonymous publisher; printer markings: Germany; circa 1934; no notice of copyright. $8.00 – 12.00.

Flat valentine; anonymous publisher; printer markings: Printed in Germany; circa 1934; no notice of copyright. $8.00 – 12.00.

Flat valentine; anonymous publisher; printer markings: Printed in Germany; circa 1930s; no notice of copyright. $6.00 – 9.00.

Chapter 17: 1930 ~ 1939 Flat Cards

Fold open valentine; anonymous publisher; printer markings: Made in U.S.A.; circa 1930s; no notice of copyright. $6.00 – 9.00.

Fold open valentine; anonymous publisher; printer markings: Made in U.S.A.; circa 1930s; no notice of copyright. $6.00 – 9.00.

Fold open valentine; anonymous publisher; printer markings: none; circa 1930s; no notice of copyright. $6.00 – 9.00.

Fold open valentine; anonymous publisher; printer markings: none; circa 1930s; no notice of copyright. $6.00 – 9.00.

1935

Flat valentine; anonymous publisher; printer markings: Printed in U.S.AM.; 1935; no notice of copyright. $6.00 – 9.00.

Back view of the heart.

Fold open valentine; anonymous publisher; printer markings: Made in U.S.A.; 1935; no notice of copyright. $6.00 – 9.00.

Flat valentine; anonymous publisher; printer markings: none; 1935; no notice of copyright. $6.00 – 9.00.

Flat valentine; anonymous publisher; printer markings: Made in U.S.A.; 1935; no notice of copyright. $6.00 – 9.00.

Flat valentine; anonymous publisher; printer markings: none; 1935; no notice of copyright. $6.00 – 9.00.

Fold open valentine; anonymous publisher; printer markings: none; circa 1935; no notice of copyright. $6.00 – 9.00.

Fold open valentine; anonymous publisher; printer markings: Made in U.S.A.; circa 1930s; no notice of copyright. $6.00 – 9.00.

Fold open valentine; anonymous publisher; printer markings: none; circa 1930s; no notice of copyright. $6.00 – 9.00.

Fold open valentine; anonymous publisher; printer markings: Made in U.S.A.; circa 1930s; no notice of copyright. $8.00 – 10.00.

Flat valentine; anonymous publisher; printer markings: none; circa 1935; no notice of copyright. $6.00 – 9.00.

Fold open valentine; anonymous publisher; printer markings: none; circa 1935; no notice of copyright. $6.00 – 9.00.

Fold open valentine; anonymous publisher; printer markings: none; circa 1935; no notice of copyright. $6.00 – 9.00.

Fold open valentine; anonymous publisher; printer markings: none; circa 1935 – 1936; no notice of copyright. $6.00 – 9.00.

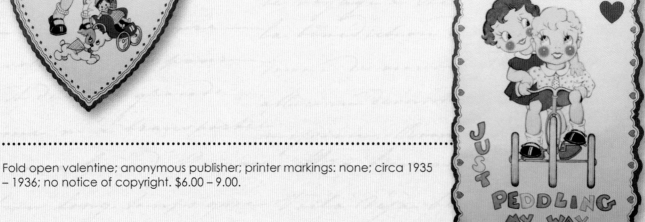

Fold open valentine; anonymous publisher; printer markings: none; circa 1935 – 1936; no notice of copyright. $6.00 – 9.00.

Fold open valentine; anonymous publisher; printer markings: none; circa 1935 – 1936; no notice of copyright. $6.00 – 9.00.

Fold open valentine; anonymous publisher; printer markings: none; circa 1935 – 1936; no notice of copyright. $6.00 – 9.00.

Fold open valentine; anonymous publisher; printer markings: none; circa 1935 – 1936; no notice of copyright. $6.00 – 9.00.

Fold open valentine; anonymous publisher; printer markings: none; circa 1920s – 1930s; no notice of copyright. $6.00 – 9.00.

Fold open valentine; anonymous publisher; printer markings: none; circa 1935 – 1936; no notice of copyright. $6.00 – 9.00.

Fold open valentine; anonymous publisher; printer markings: none; circa mid 1930s; no notice of copyright. $6.00 – 9.00.

Fold open valentine; anonymous publisher; printer markings: none; circa 1930s; no notice of copyright. $6.00 – 9.00.

Fold open valentine; anonymous publisher; printer markings: Printed in U.S.AM.; circa 1930s; no notice of copyright. $6.00 – 9.00.

Fold open valentine, back view (left) and front view (right); anonymous publisher; printer markings: Made in U.S.A.; circa 1920s – 1930s; no notice of copyright. $6.00 – 9.00.

Fold open valentine; anonymous publisher; printer markings: Printed in U.S.A.; circa 1930s; no notice of copyright. $6.00 – 9.00.

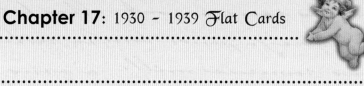

Fold open valentine; anonymous publisher; printer markings: Printed in U.S.A.; circa 1930s; no notice of copyright. $6.00 – 9.00.

Fold open valentine, front view showing boy holding a heart and valentine; anonymous publisher; printer markings: Made in U.S.A.; circa 1930s; no notice of copyright. $6.00 – 9.00.

Back view of valentine showing a girl wearing a gown holding a heart and valentine.

1936

Flat valentine; anonymous publisher; printer markings: Made in U.S.A.; 1936; no notice of copyright. $6.00 – 9.00.

Flat valentine; anonymous publisher; printer markings: none; 1936; no notice of copyright. $6.00 – 9.00.

225

Flat valentine; anonymous publisher; printer markings: Made in U.S.A.; 1936; no notice of copyright. $6.00 – 9.00.

Fold open valentine; anonymous publisher; printer markings: Made in U.S.A.; 1936; no notice of copyright. $6.00 – 9.00.

Fold open valentine; anonymous publisher; printer markings: Made in U.S.A.; 1936; no notice of copyright. $6.00 – 9.00.

Fold open valentine; anonymous publisher; printer markings: Made in U.S.A.; 1936; no notice of copyright. $6.00 – 9.00.

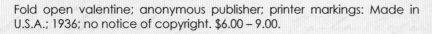

Fold open valentine; anonymous publisher; printer markings: Made in U.S.A.; 1936; no notice of copyright. $6.00 – 9.00.

Fold open valentine; anonymous publisher; printer markings: none; circa 1936; no notice of copyright. $6.00 – 9.00.

Fold open valentine; anonymous publisher; printer markings: none; 1936; no notice of copyright. $6.00 – 9.00.

Fold open valentine; anonymous publisher; printer markings: none; circa 1936 – early 1940s; no notice of copyright. $6.00 – 9.00.

Fold open valentine; anonymous publisher; printer markings: Made in U.S.A.; circa 1936 – early 1940s; no notice of copyright. $6.00 – 9.00.

Fold open valentine, "Do You Glove Me?"; anonymous publisher: printer markings: Made in U.S.A.; circa 1936; no notice of copyright. $6.00 – 9.00.

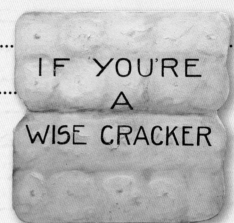

Fold open valentine; anonymous publisher; printer markings: none; circa 1936; no notice of copyright. $6.00 – 9.00.

Fold open valentine; anonymous publisher; printer markings: none; circa 1936; no notice of copyright. $6.00 – 9.00.

Fold open valentine; anonymous publisher; printer markings: Made in U.S.A. Series 1254; circa 1936 – early 1940s; no notice of copyright. $6.00 – 9.00.

Flat valentine; anonymous publisher; printer markings: Made in U.S.A.; circa 1930s; no notice of copyright. $6.00 – 9.00.

Fold open valentine; anonymous publisher; printer markings: none; circa 1936 – early 1940s; no notice of copyright. $6.00 – 9.00.

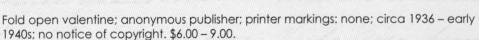

Fold open valentine; anonymous publisher; printer markings: Made in U.S.A.; 1936; no notice of copyright. $6.00 – 9.00.

Flat valentine; anonymous publisher; printer markings: Made in U.S.A.; circa 1936; no notice of copyright. $6.00 – 9.00.

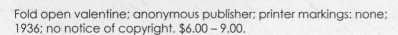

Fold open valentine; anonymous publisher; printer markings: Made in U.S.A.; 1936; no notice of copyright. $6.00 – 9.00.

Fold open valentine; anonymous publisher; printer markings: none; 1936; no notice of copyright. $6.00 – 9.00.

Fold open valentine; anonymous publisher; printer markings: Made in U.S.A.; 1936; no notice of copyright. $6.00 – 9.00.

Fold open valentine; anonymous publisher; printer markings: Made in U.S.A.; 1936; no notice of copyright. $6.00 – 9.00.

Fold open valentine; anonymous publisher; printer markings: Printed In U.S. AMER.; circa 1936; no notice of copyright. $6.00 – 9.00.

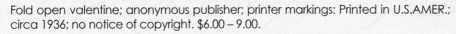

Fold open valentine; anonymous publisher; printer markings: Printed in U.S.AMER.; circa 1936; no notice of copyright. $6.00 – 9.00.

Flat rebus valentine, an inscription where some of the words are replaced by pictures for the reader to decipher; anonymous publisher; printer markings: none; circa 1930s; no notice of copyright. $6.00 – 9.00.

Flat valentine; anonymous publisher; printer markings: none; circa 1936; no notice of copyright. $6.00 – 9.00.

Fold open valentine; anonymous publisher; printer markings: Printed in U.S. AMER.; circa 1936; no notice of copyright. $6.00 – 9.00.

Fold open valentine; anonymous publisher; printer markings: Made in U.S.A.; 1936; no notice of copyright. $6.00 – 9.00.

1937

Flat valentine; anonymous publisher; printer markings: Made in U.S.A.; 1937; no notice of copyright. $6.00 – 9.00.

Fold open valentine; anonymous publisher; printer markings: Printed in U.S.AM.; 1937; no notice of copyright. $6.00 – 9.00.

Fold open valentine; anonymous publisher; printer markings: Made in U.S.A.; circa 1937; no notice of copyright. $6.00 – 9.00.

Chapter 17: 1930 – 1939 Flat Cards

Fold open valentine; anonymous publisher; printer markings: Made in U.S.A.; circa 1937; no notice of copyright. $6.00 – 9.00.

Flat valentine; anonymous publisher; printer markings: Made in U.S.A.; 1937; no notice of copyright. $6.00 – 9.00.

Flat valentine; anonymous publisher; printer markings: Made in U.S.A.; 1937; no notice of copyright. $6.00 – 9.00.

Flat valentine; anonymous publisher; printer markings: Made in U.S.A.; 1937; no notice of copyright. $6.00 – 9.00.

Fold open valentine; anonymous publisher; printer markings: Made in U.S.A.; circa 1930s; no notice of copyright. $6.00 – 9.00.

Fold open valentine; anonymous publisher; printer markings: Made in U.S.A.; circa 1937; no notice of copyright. $6.00 – 9.00.

Flat valentine; anonymous publisher; printer markings: Made in U.S. AM.; circa 1930s; no notice of copyright. $10.00 – 15.00.

Flat valentine; anonymous publisher; printer markings: none; circa 1930s; no notice of copyright. $6.00 – 9.00.

Flat valentine; anonymous publisher; printer markings: Made in Germany; circa 1930s; no notice of copyright. $6.00 – 9.00.

Flat valentine; anonymous publisher; printer markings: Made in U.S.A.; circa 1930s; no notice of copyright. $6.00 – 9.00.

Fold open valentine; anonymous publisher; printer markings: Printed in U.S.A.; circa late 1920s – 1930s; no notice of copyright. $6.00 – 9.00.

Fold open valentine; anonymous publisher; printer markings: Made in U.S.A.; circa 1930s; no notice of copyright. $6.00 – 9.00.

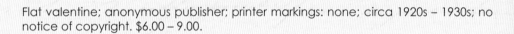

Flat valentine; anonymous publisher; printer markings: none; circa 1920s – 1930s; no notice of copyright. $6.00 – 9.00.

1938

Fold open valentine; anonymous publisher; printer markings: Made in U.S.A.; 1938; no notice of copyright. $6.00 – 9.00.

Fold open valentine; anonymous publisher; printer markings: none; 1938; no notice of copyright. $6.00 – 9.00.

Flat valentine; anonymous publisher; printer markings: Made in U.S.A.; circa 1938; no notice of copyright. $6.00 – 9.00.

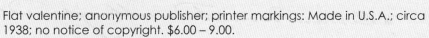

Flat valentine; anonymous publisher; printer markings: Made in U.S.A.; circa 1938; no notice of copyright. $6.00 – 9.00.

Flat valentine; anonymous publisher; printer markings: none; circa 1930s; no notice of copyright. $6.00 – 9.00.

Flat valentine; anonymous publisher; printer markings: Made in U.S.A.; circa 1930s; no notice of copyright. $6.00 – 9.00.

1939

Fold open valentine; anonymous publisher; printer markings: Made in U.S. AM.; 1939; no notice of copyright. $6.00 – 9.00.

Flat valentine; anonymous publisher; printer markings: Made in U.S.A.; 1939; no notice of copyright. $6.00 – 9.00.

Chapter 18
1930 ~ 1939
Fold Down Cards

America's protectionism of growing industry protected our greeting card businesss against the stiff competition of inexpensive German products made by workers who earned lower wages. The Smoot-Hawley Tariff of June 1930 made it a requirement for countries to clearly mark in English the place where their goods were made.[133] Fold down valentines were now clearly marked as American in origin. These cards are the choice of American children and adults when it came to presenting valentines through the Great Depression.

Anonymously Published Card
Markings Indicating Place of Manufacture or Printing

- "Made in Germany"

- "Made in U.S.A."

Types of Valentines Illustrated

- Fold down valentines
- Fold out valentines

Design Features Illustrated

- Cartoon style characters
- Die-cut features
- Primary color themes

Subjects Illustrated

- Bathtub girls
- Beach scenes
- Card playing
- Cars
- Cartoon style children
- Clowns
- Cottages
- Dogs
- Ducks
- Dutch children
- Gardening
- Musicians
- Newsboys
- Outdoor scenes
- Pirates
- Police officers
- Puppet theaters
- Safes
- Scarecrows
- Thieves

Exact years in captions are original sender/receiver dates.

Fold down valentine; anonymous publisher; printer markings: Made in U.S.A.; circa late 1920s – early 1930s; no notice of copyright. $8.00 – 12.00.

Fold down valentine; anonymous publisher; printer markings: Made in U.S.AM.; circa late 1920s – early 1930s; no notice of copyright. $8.00 – 12.00.

Fold down valentine; anonymous publisher; printer markings: Made in U.S.A.; circa late 1920s – early 1930s; no notice of copyright. $8.00 – 12.00.

1930

Fold down valentine; anonymous publisher; printer markings: none; 1930; no notice of copyright. $12.00 – 15.00.

1931

Fold down valentine; anonymous publisher; printer markings: Printed in Germany; 1931; no notice of copyright. $8.00 – 12.00.

1932

Fold out valentine; anonymous publisher; printer markings: none; circa 1932; no notice of copyright. $8.00 – 10.00.

Fold out valentine; anonymous publisher; printer markings: Made in U.S.A.; circa 1932; no notice of copyright. $8.00 – 10.00.

Fold out valentine; anonymous publisher; printer markings: none; circa 1932; no notice of copyright. $8.00 – 10.00.

Fold down valentine; anonymous publisher; printer markings: Made in U.S.A.; circa mid 1930s; no notice of copyright. $6.00 – 9.00.

Fold out valentine; anonymous publisher; printer markings: none; circa mid 1930s; no notice of copyright. $8.00 – 10.00.

Fold out valentine; anonymous publisher; printer markings: Made in U.S.A.; circa early to mid 1930s; no notice of copyright. $6.00 – 9.00.

Fold out valentine; anonymous publisher; printer markings: Made in U.S.A.; circa early to middle of the 1930s; no notice of copyright. $6.00 – 9.00.

1933

Fold down valentine; anonymous publisher; printer markings: Printed in Germany; 1933; no notice of copyright. $15.00 – 25.00.

1934

Fold down valentine; anonymous publisher; printer markings: Printed in Germany; circa 1934 – 1936; no notice of copyright. $6.00 – 9.00.

1935

Fold out valentine; anonymous publisher; printer markings: Made in U.S.A.; 1935; no notice of copyright. $8.00 – 10.00.

Fold out valentine; anonymous publisher; printer markings: none; circa mid 1930s; no notice of copyright. $6.00 – 9.00.

Fold out valentine; anonymous publisher; printer markings: none; circa mid 1930s; no notice of copyright. $10.00 – 14.00.

Fold down valentine; anonymous publisher; printer markings: Made in U.S.A.; circa mid 1930s; no notice of copyright. $6.00 – 9.00.

Fold out valentine; anonymous publisher; printer markings: none; circa mid 1930s; no notice of copyright. $6.00 – 9.00.

Fold out valentine; anonymous publisher; printer markings: none; circa mid 1930s; no notice of copyright. $6.00 – 9.00.

Fold down valentine; anonymous publisher; printer markings: none; circa 1930s; no notice of copyright. $8.00 – 14.00.

Open card view showing bathtub interior.

Fold down valentine; anonymous publisher; printer markings: none; circa 1930s; no notice of copyright. $8.00 – 14.00.

Open card view showing bathtub interior.

241

Fold down valentine; anonymous publisher; printer markings: none; circa 1930s; no notice of copyright. $8.00 – 14.00.

Open card view showing rowboat interior.

1936

Fold down valentine; anonymous publisher; printer markings: Made in U.S.A.; 1936; no notice of copyright. $6.00 – 9.00.

Fold out valentine; anonymous publisher; printer markings: Made in U.S.A.; circa 1936; no notice of copyright. $10.00 – 14.00.

Fold out valentine; anonymous publisher; printer markings: none; 1936; no notice of copyright. $10.00 – 14.00.

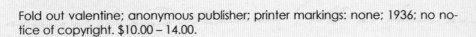

Fold out valentine; anonymous publisher; printer markings: Printed in U.S.AM.; 1936; no notice of copyright. $6.00 – 9.00.

Fold out valentine; anonymous publisher; printer markings: none; 1936; no notice of copyright. $10.00 – 14.00.

Fold out valentine; anonymous publisher; printer markings: Made in U.S.A.; circa 1936; no notice of copyright. $6.00 – 9.00.

Fold out valentine; anonymous publisher; printer markings: Made in U.S.A.; circa 1930s; no notice of copyright. $6.00 – 9.00.

Fold out valentine; anonymous publisher; printer markings: none; circa 1930s; no notice of copyright. $6.00 – 9.00.

Fold out valentine; anonymous publisher; printer markings: none; circa 1930s; no notice of copyright. $6.00 – 9.00.

1937

Fold down valentine; anonymous publisher; printer markings: Printed in Germany; circa 1937; no notice of copyright. $6.00 – 9.00.

1938

Fold out valentine; anonymous publisher; printer markings: Made in U.S.A.; 1938; no notice of copyright. $10.00 – 14.00.

Fold out valentine; anonymous publisher; printer markings: none; 1938; no notice of copyright. $10.00 – 14.00.

1939

Fold out valentine; anonymous publisher; printer markings: Made in U.S.A.; circa 1939; no notice of copyright. $8.00 – 10.00.

Fold out valentine; anonymous publisher; printer markings: Made in U.S.A.; circa 1930s; no notice of copyright. $6.00 – 9.00.

Fold out valentine; anonymous publisher; printer markings: Printed in U.S. AM.; circa 1930s; no notice of copyright. $6.00 – 9.00.

Fold down valentine; anonymous publisher; printer markings: Made in U.S.A.; circa 1930s – 1940s; no notice of copyright. $10.00 – 15.00.

Fold down valentine; anonymous publisher; printer markings: Made in U.S.A.; circa 1930s – 1940s; no notice of copyright. $10.00 – 15.00.

Chapter 19
1930 ~ 1939
Mechanical Cards

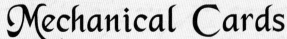

Americans continued to be fond of mechanical valentines through the thirties. Maybe it was a fun way to alleviate the burden of the Great Depression. Fascination with these cards continued and they undoubtedly became a popular amusement for children. Innovation and clever designs of the period are now predominantly the product of American card companies and to a lesser extent German makers. Americans begin buying American-made cards of unique artistic quality. Now American greeting card industries had come into their own. American industries emerged, developed, and thrived in a commercial and artistic sense to usher Americans through a decade of struggles and deprivations.

Anonymously Published Card
Markings Indicating Place of Manufacture or Printing

- "Germany"
- "Made in Germany"
- "Printed in Germany"

Types of Valentines Illustrated

- Mechanical valentines

Design Features Illustrated

- Primary color schemes
- Thin paper
- Yellow green-themed color scheme

Subjects Illustrated

- Bears
- Blimps
- Books
- Carriages
- Cars
- Cartoon style characters
- Cats
- Children
- Clowns
- Cottages
- Dogs
- Ducks
- Elephants
- Elves
- Flower girls
- Funny faces
- Garden cottages
- Gardening
- Gardens
- Goats
- Google-eyed children
- Kite flying
- Lions
- Motorcycles
- Moveable eyes
- Musicians
- Nursery rhyme characters
- Old-fashioned girls
- Planes
- Police officers
- Policemen
- Radio operators
- Sailors
- Scissors
- Ships
- Telephone calls
- Typists
- Umbrellas
- Zeppelins

Anonymously Published Cards Not Illustrated

Card has a value of $15.00 – 20.00.

- 1935 African American girl with moveable eyes, yellow dress with red polka dots

Published Cards Not Illustrated

C. Co., Made in USA
Cards have a value of $9.00 – 14.00 each.
- 1930s Humpty Dumpty, mechanical
- 1930s Peter, Peter Pumpkin Eater, mechanical

Charles Twelvetrees, "CT" artist signature
Cards have a value of $15.00 – 25.00 each.
- 1930s – 1940s elephant, mechanical, Made in U.S.A., "CT" artist signature
- 1930s dog and cat with bonnet, "I think you're swell," Made in U.S.A., "CT" artist signature

Exact years in captions are original sender/receiver dates.

1930

Mechanical valentine, cupid and girl move; anonymous publisher; printer markings: Germany; 1930; no notice of copyright. $15.00 – 20.00.

1931

Mechanical valentine, legs move; anonymous publisher; printer markings: Germany; 1931; no notice of copyright. $15.00 – 20.00.

1932

Mechanical valentine (damaged head), boat and swimmer move; anonymous publisher; printer markings: Printed in Germany; 1932; no notice of copyright. $8.00 – 12.00.

Mechanical valentine, eyes and ear move; publisher: none; printer markings: Made in U.S.A. $5.00 – 8.00.

1933

Mechanical valentine, flower hat moves; anonymous publisher; printer markings: none; circa 1933; no notice of copyright. $8.00 – 12.00.

View when flower hat is pulled up.

Mechanical valentine, flower hat moves; anonymous publisher; printer markings: none; 1933; no notice of copyright. $8.00 – 12.00.

1934

Mechanical valentine, boy moves; anonymous publisher; printer markings: Printed in Germany; 1934; no notice of copyright. $10.00 – 13.00.

1935

Mechanical valentine, legs move; anonymous publisher; printer markings: Made in Germany; 1935; no notice of copyright. $13.00 – 20.00.

Mechanical valentine, eyes move; anonymous publisher; printer markings: none; 1935; no notice of copyright. $13.00 – 16.00.

Mechanical valentine, head moves; anonymous publisher; printer markings: none; circa 1930s; no notice of copyright. $9.00 – 13.00.

Mechanical valentine, hat moves; anonymous publisher; printer markings: none; circa 1930s; no notice of copyright. $9.00 – 13.00.

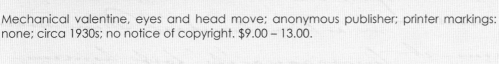

Mechanical valentine, eyes and head move; anonymous publisher; printer markings: none; circa 1930s; no notice of copyright. $9.00 – 13.00.

Mechanical valentine, head moves; anonymous publisher; printer markings: none; 1935; no notice of copyright. $8.00 – 12.00.

Chapter 19: 1930 – 1939 Mechanical Cards

Mechanical valentine, eyes move; anonymous publisher; printer markings: none; circa 1930s; no notice of copyright. $20.00 – 25.00.

Mechanical valentine, arm and eyes move; anonymous publisher; printer markings: none; circa 1930s; no notice of copyright. $20.00 – 25.00.

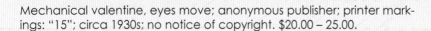

Mechanical valentine, eyes move; anonymous publisher; printer markings: "15"; circa 1930s; no notice of copyright. $20.00 – 25.00.

Mechanical valentine, eyes move; anonymous publisher; printer markings: none; circa 1930s; no notice of copyright. $9.00 – 13.00.

Mechanical valentine, eyes move; anonymous publisher; printer markings: none; circa 1930s; no notice of copyright. $15.00 – 20.00.

Mechanical valentine, eyes move; anonymous publisher; printer markings: none; circa 1930s; no notice of copyright. $9.00 – 13.00.

1936

Mechanical valentine, sheep skin moves; anonymous publisher; printer markings: Made in U.S.A.; 1936; no notice of copyright. $20.00 – 25.00.

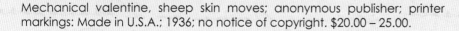

Mechanical valentine, motorcycle moves; anonymous publisher; printer markings: Made in U.S.A.; circa 1930s – 1940s; no notice of copyright. $20.00 – 25.00.

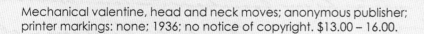

Mechanical valentine, head and neck moves; anonymous publisher; printer markings: none; 1936; no notice of copyright. $13.00 – 16.00.

Mechanical valentine, figure moves; anonymous publisher; printer markings: Made in U.S.A.; 1936; no notice of copyright. $13.00 – 16.00.

Mechanical valentine, head moves; anonymous publisher; printer markings: Made in Germany; circa 1930s; no notice of copyright. $9.00 – 13.00.

Mechanical valentine, head moves; anonymous publisher; printer markings: Made in Germany; circa 1936; no notice of copyright. $13.00 – 16.00.

1938

Mechanical valentine, facial expressions change, view shows winking girl; anonymous publisher; printer markings: none; 1938; no notice of copyright. $15.00 – 20.00.

View shows girl smiling.

Mechanical valentine, facial expression changes, view shows smiling girl; anonymous publisher; printer markings: Made in U.S.A.; circa 1930s; no notice of copyright. $15.00 – 20.00.

View shows girl frowning.

Mechanical valentine, book moves; anonymous publisher; printer markings: Germany; circa 1930s; no notice of copyright. $9.00 – 13.00.

Mechanical valentine, upper body moves; anonymous publisher; printer markings: Made in U.S.A.; circa 1930s; no notice of copyright. $9.00 – 13.00.

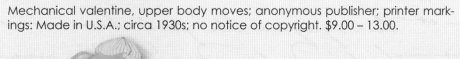

Mechanical valentine, goat and riders move; anonymous publisher; printer markings: none; circa 1930s; no notice of copyright. $9.00 – 13.00.

Mechanical valentine, typewriter paper moves; anonymous publisher; printer markings: Made in U.S.A.; circa 1930s; no notice of copyright. $9.00 – 13.00.

Mechanical valentine, rider moves; anonymous publisher; printer markings: Made in U.S.A.; circa 1930s; no notice of copyright. $9.00 – 13.00.

Mechanical valentine, tongue and eyes move; anonymous publisher; printer markings: Germany; circa mid 1930s; no notice of copyright. $20.00 – 30.00.

Mechanical valentine, scissors move; anonymous publisher; printer markings: Made in U.S.A.; circa 1930s; no notice of copyright. $9.00 – 13.00.

Mechanical valentine, girl's face moves; anonymous publisher; printer markings: Made in Germany; circa 1920s – 1930s; no notice of copyright. $9.00 – 13.00.

Mechanical valentine, neck and head move; anonymous publisher; printer markings: Made in Germany; circa 1920s – 1930s; no notice of copyright. $9.00 – 13.00.

Mechanical valentine, tongue and eyes move; anonymous publisher; printer markings: Printed in Germany; circa 1920s – 1930s; no notice of copyright. $20.00 – 25.00.

Mechanical valentine, eyes and arm move; anonymous publisher; printer markings: Printed in Germany; circa 1920s – 1930s; no notice of copyright. $20.00 – 25.00.

Mechanical valentine, door and window open; anonymous publisher; printer markings: none; circa 1930s; no notice of copyright. $9.00 – 13.00.

Mechanical valentine, girl's head moves; anonymous publisher; printer markings: Made in U.S.A.; circa 1930s; no notice of copyright. $9.00 – 13.00.

Chapter 19: 1930 – 1939 Mechanical Cards

Mechanical valentine, head moves; anonymous publisher; printer markings: Germany; circa 1930s; no notice of copyright. $9.00 – 13.00.

Mechanical valentine, duck bill moves; anonymous publisher; printer markings: Made in U.S.A.; circa 1930s; no notice of copyright. $9.00 – 13.00.

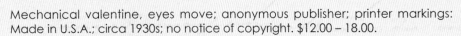

Mechanical valentine, eyes move; anonymous publisher; printer markings: Made in U.S.A.; circa 1930s; no notice of copyright. $12.00 – 18.00.

Mechanical valentine, arm moves; anonymous publisher; printer markings: none; circa 1930s; no notice of copyright. $15.00 – 20.00.

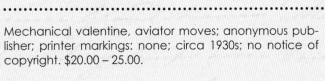

Mechanical valentine, aviator moves; anonymous publisher; printer markings: none; circa 1930s; no notice of copyright. $20.00 – 25.00.

Mechanical valentine, girl moves; anonymous publisher; printer markings: Made in U.S.A.; circa 1930s; no notice of copyright. $15.00 – 20.00.

Mechanical valentine, eyes move; anonymous publisher; printer markings: Printed in Germany; circa 1920s – 1930s; no notice of copyright. $10.00 – 15.00.

Mechanical valentine, couple moves; anonymous publisher; printer markings: Made in U.S. AM.; circa 1930s; no notice of copyright. $20.00 – 25.00.

Mechanical valentine, upper body moves; anonymous publisher; printer markings: Made in Germany; circa 1930s; no notice of copyright. $20.00 – 25.00.

Mechanical valentine, leg moves; anonymous publisher; printer markings: none; circa 1930s; no notice of copyright. $7.00 – 13.00.

Mechanical valentine, bow and arm move; anonymous publisher; printer markings: none; circa 1930s; no notice of copyright. $7.00 – 13.00.

Mechanical valentine, head moves; anonymous publisher; printer markings: Made in Germany; circa 1930s; no notice of copyright. $9.00 – 13.00.

Mechanical valentine, aviator moves; anonymous publisher; printer markings: Made in Germany; circa 1930s; no notice of copyright. $20.00 – 25.00.

Mechanical valentine, head moves; anonymous publisher; printer markings: Made in U.S.A.; circa 1930s; no notice of copyright. $9.00 – 13.00.

Chapter 20
1940 ~ 1949
Flat Cards

Valentine cards in the 1940s epitomized all that was great and fanciful in the minds of Americans at war. Children perpetuated the custom of valentine exchanges. Great companies listed below made stunning examples of American cards. American greeting card companies continued to dominate the scene when the nation was at war and in the years afterwards. Valentine collectors will appreciate the deprivations Americans faced when they examine the paper quality of 1940s valentines. Greeting cards of the period show indication of paper and other supply shortages due to the wartime economy. Patriotism and military themes were among the decade's favorite valentine subjects.

Types of Valentines Illustrated

- Flat valentines
- Fold open valentines
- Fold out valentines

Design Features Illustrated

- Antiqued or yellowish appearance
- Cardboard type paper
- Paper easel tabs
- Primary colors

Subjects Illustrated

- Anthropomorphism
- Baseball
- Bears
- Boys
- Cats
- Children
- Dogs
- Elephants
- Farmers
- Lions
- Military themes
- Musicians
- Nurses
- Parrots
- Postmen
- Soldiers
- Teachers

Published Cards Not Illustrated

A.C. Co., *Product of U.S.A*
Cards have a value of $3.00 – 6.00 each.
- 1940s boy proposing
- 1940s cowboy with lasso
- 1940s farmer and girl in cabbage patch, fold out
- 1940s hobo and dog, fold out
- 1940s two bluebirds
- 1942 dog with message

American Greetings, *Cleveland, Ohio*
Cards have a value of $3.00 – 6.00 each.
- 1940s – 1950s bear driving car
- 1940s anthropomorphic lamps
- 1940s anthropomorphic sugar bowl
- 1940s bunny
- 1940s cannon and soldier
- 1940s dog pole vaulting
- 1940s dog, Pekinese
- 1940s girl with moveable eyes
- 1940s Indian squaw in teepee
- 1945 – 1947 flamenco dancer
- 1945 – 1947 pink flowers, heart, gray stripe
- 1945 – 1947 children, teacher valentine

Americard
Cards have a value of $5.00 – 9.00 each.
- 1940s angel bear
- 1940s bear with first aid
- 1940s book in heart, teacher card
- 1940s boy and "To My Teacher"
- 1940s boy

Chapter 20: 1940 ~ 1949 Flat Cards

- 1940s boy on clouds
- 1940s boy with bubble pile
- 1940s boy with dog, fold out
- 1940s boy with blow torch
- 1940s boy with milk bottle
- 1940s boy with puppies in heart
- 1940s boy with wolf mask
- 1940s boy with fiddle
- 1940s cat sweeping
- 1940s children on seesaw
- 1940s couple
- 1940s girl painting sign
- 1940s couple of kids on swing
- 1940s couple on go cart
- 1940s couple with children, "Don't be chicken heart-ed"
- 1940s couple, flower basket, teacher
- 1940s dog playing tennis
- 1940s dog with carrot
- 1940s fold out children in school
- 1940s fold out soldier girl
- 1940s fold out, chef and girl, "Be my honey bun, be my dream"
- 1940s fold up farmer boy
- 1940s girl with puppy, fold up
- 1940s girl on scale with kitten
- 1940s girl with cowboy
- 1940s girl, lace heart
- 1940s girl, teacher card
- 1940s heart shape, boy with slingshot, teacher card
- 1940s heart, arrow
- 1940s heart, boy, and three puppies
- 1940s hula dancer
- 1940s mechanical card, sky diving
- 1940s mechanical girl, double chin
- 1940s orchid
- 1940s pirate and girl
- 1940s puppy and record, google applied moving eye
- 1940s red heart teacher card
- 1940s sailor and girl
- 1940s sailor bear in boat
- 1940s small heart, lace overlay, teacher card
- 1940s teddy and honey pot
- 1940s two hearts, teacher, school house
- 1942 boy in boat, Made in USA
- 1942 fold down girl picking heart apples, Made in USA
- 1942 girl walking two dogs, Made in USA
- 1944 mechanical card, dog in doghouse
- 1945 boy with three dogs, "I'll go to the dogs"

C. Co., Made in USA
Cards have a value of $3.00 – 6.00 each.
- 1940s boy on wooden go cart
- 1941 girl with big eyes, flower basket

Carrington
Cards have a value of $5.00 – 12.00 each.
Trademark tree outline with E, A, or H inside.
- 1940s bear blows bubbles
- 1940s bear cub
- 1940s bears on sled
- 1940s boy goes nuts
- 1940s boy with puppet
- 1940s children roller skating
- 1940s fan
- 1940s old-fashioned couple
- 1940s old-fashioned couple in garden
- 1940s soldier and nurse in jeep
- 1940s sugar and spice couple
- 1942 mechanical, girl with ukulele
- 1942 private boy
- 1944 tough boy in blue overalls

Charles Twelvetrees, "CT" artist signature
Cards have a value of $6.00 – 12.00 each.
- 1940s mechanical, cat and dog, Made in U.S.A., "CT" artist signature

DA, Made in U.S.A.
Cards have a value of $3.00 – 6.00 each.
- 1945 – 1947 birdhouse and birds

Double Glo
Cards have a value of $6.00 – 12.00 each.
- 1940s "To My Beloved" flowers, note
- 1940s boy scared in bed, "Who dun nit?"
- 1940s boy with yellow curtains in heart, flowers, "Hung out my shingle," heart specialist
- 1940s cowgirl with lasso, Made in USA
- 1940s duck majorette, "I'd like to lead a big parade," Made in USA
- 1940s dunce, "For teacher"
- 1940s girl in heart with giant scissor, "cut it out, can't you see you were just cut out for me," Made in USA
- 1940s girl in long gown plucking sunflowers, "I'm pickin' petals from posies"
- 1940s heart, flowers
- 1940s memo pad, flowers, "For teacher"
- 1940s pirate treasure
- 1940s red lace and flowers

F. & Co. in Heart, Made in U.S.A.
Cards have a value of $3.00 – 6.00 each.
- 1945 – 1947 desk, teacher

F. &. Co., Made in U.S.A.
Cards have a value of $3.00 – 6.00 each.
- 1940s – 1950s two kittens in heart, teacher valentine, Made in U.S.A.

Chapter 20: 1940 – 1949 *Flat Cards*

Forget Me Not Greeting Cards

Cards have a value of $3.00 – 6.00 each.
- 1945 – 1947 book card, hearts and flowers

Gibson Cincinnati, U.S.A.

Cards have a value of $6.00 – 12.00 each.
- 1940s dog, "Doggone lonesome"
- 1940s history book, Adam and Eve

Golden Bell

Cards have a value of $3.00 – 6.00 each.
- 1940s bear with pencil, "Dear Teacher," bell with GB inside
- 1940s couple in orchard
- 1940s cellophane, lace and silver fan and flower, GB in box, Made in USA
- 1940s heart-shaped bear in bed
- 1940s hunter and deer head, applied birch trees, Golden Bell logo, blue print, Made in USA
- 1940s squirrel
- 1940s two kittens, Made in USA

Hallmark

Cards have a value of $8.00 – 12.00 each.
- 1940s couple in bicycle built for two
- 1944 bleeding hearts and roses, teacher card
- 1944 satin red heart card
- 1945 cocker spaniels
- 1946 heart cutout
- 1946 hobby horse, teacher card
- 1946 rose in black heart
- 1947 envelope with graphics
- 1947 girl in picture hat
- 1947 kitten, "For Teacher"

- 1947 roses and flowers
- 1948 goofy guy with old fashioned bathing suit
- 1948 turtle

J.S. Publishing Company, New York

Cards have a value of $3.00 – 6.00 each.
- 1945 – 1947 pink flower arrangement
- 1945 – 1947 teapot and flowers

Merlye

Cards have a value of $3.00 – 6.00 each.
- 1945 – 1947 heart, bouquets
- 1945 – 1947 pink hearts, dogwood

Norcross, New York

Cards have a value of $3.00 – 9.00 each.
- 1940s bear on books, teacher
- 1940s bear with heart
- 1940s cat distressed with bouquet

Q – Made in U.S.A.

Cards have a value of $3.00 – 6.00 each.
- 1945 – 1947 heart, music notes
- 1945 – 1947 girl radio operator

Quality Card

Cards have a value of $3.00 – 6.00 each.
- 1940s Scottie dogs, Made in USA

Rust Craft, Boston, USA

Cards have a value of $6.00 – 9.00 each.
- 1940s old-fashioned couple entering shop
- 1946 heart and flowers

Exact years in captions are original sender/receiver dates.

1940

Flat valentine; anonymous publisher; printer markings: Made in U.S.A.; 1940; no notice of copyright. $3.00 – 8.00.

1941

Fold open card; anonymous publisher; printer markings: Made in U.S.A.; 1941; no notice of copyright. $3.00 – 8.00.

1942

Flat valentine; anonymous publisher; printer markings: Made in U.S.A.; 1942; no notice of copyright. $3.00 – 8.00.

Flat valentine with easel; anonymous publisher; printer markings: Made in U.S.A.; circa 1942; no notice of copyright. $3.00 – 8.00.

Flat valentine with easel; anonymous publisher; printer markings: Made in U.S.A.; 1942; no notice of copyright. $3.00 – 8.00.

Flat valentine; anonymous publisher; printer markings: none; 1942; no notice of copyright. $3.00 – 8.00.

Fold open valentine; anonymous publisher; printer markings: Printed in U.S.A.; circa 1942; no notice of copyright. $3.00 – 8.00.

Flat valentine with easel; anonymous publisher; printer markings: Made in U.S.A.; circa 1942; no notice of copyright. $3.00 – 8.00.

1943

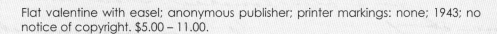

Flat valentine with easel; anonymous publisher; printer markings: none; 1943; no notice of copyright. $5.00 – 11.00.

Flat valentine with easel; anonymous publisher; printer markings: Made in U.S.A.; 1943; no notice of copyright. $3.00 – 8.00.

Chapter 20: 1940 – 1949 Flat Cards

Flat valentine with easel; anonymous publisher; printer markings: Made in U.S.A.; 1943; no notice of copyright. $3.00 – 8.00.

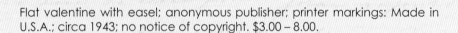

Flat valentine with easel; anonymous publisher; printer markings: Made in U.S.A.; 1943; no notice of copyright. $3.00 – 8.00.

Flat valentine with easel; anonymous publisher; printer markings: Made in U.S.A.; circa 1943; no notice of copyright. $3.00 – 8.00.

Flat valentine with easel; anonymous publisher; printer markings: Made in U.S.A.; circa 1943; no notice of copyright. $3.00 – 8.00.

Flat valentine with easel; anonymous publisher; printer markings: Made in U.S.A.; 1943; no notice of copyright. $3.00 – 8.00.

1944

Flat valentine with easel; anonymous publisher; printer markings: Made in U.S.A.; 1944; no notice of copyright. $3.00 – 8.00.

Flat valentine with easel; anonymous publisher; printer markings: none; 1944; no notice of copyright. $3.00 – 8.00.

1945

Flat valentine with easel; anonymous publisher; printer markings: Made in U.S.A.; 1945; no notice of copyright. $5.00 – 11.00.

Flat valentine with easel; anonymous publisher; printer markings: Made in U.S.A.; 1945; no notice of copyright. $3.00 – 8.00.

Flat valentine with easel; anonymous publisher; printer markings: Made in U.S.A.; 1945; no notice of copyright. $3.00 – 8.00.

1945 – 1947

Flat valentine; anonymous publisher; printer markings: Made in U.S.A.; circa 1945 – 1947; no notice of copyright. $3.00 – 8.00.

Flat valentine; anonymous publisher; printer markings: Made in U.S.A.; 1945; no notice of copyright. $3.00 – 8.00.

Flat valentine with easel; anonymous publisher; printer markings: Made in U.S.A.; circa 1940s; no notice of copyright. $3.00 – 8.00.

Flat valentine; anonymous publisher; printer markings: Made in U.S.A.; circa 1945 – 1947; no notice of copyright. $3.00 – 8.00.

Flat valentine; anonymous publisher; printer markings: Made in U.S.A.; circa 1945 – 1947; no notice of copyright. $3.00 – 8.00.

1949

Flat valentine; anonymous publisher; printer markings: none; 1949; no notice of copyright. $3.00 – 8.00.

Flat valentine; anonymous publisher; printer markings: Made in U.S.A.; circa 1940s; no notice of copyright. $5.00 – 11.00.

Flat valentine; anonymous publisher; printer markings: Made in U.S.A.; circa 1940s; no notice of copyright. $5.00 – 11.00.

Flat valentine with easel; anonymous publisher; printer markings: Made in U.S.A.; circa 1940s; no notice of copyright. $3.00 – 8.00.

Flat valentine with easel; anonymous publisher; printer markings: Made in U.S.A.; circa 1940s; no notice of copyright. $3.00 – 8.00.

Flat valentine; anonymous publisher; printer markings: none; circa 1940s; no notice of copyright. $3.00 – 8.00.

Flat valentine with easel; anonymous publisher; printer markings: Made in U.S.A.; circa 1940s; no notice of copyright. $3.00 – 8.00.

Flat valentine with moveable eye; anonymous publisher; printer markings: none; circa 1940s; no notice of copyright. $3.00 – 8.00.

Flat valentine; anonymous publisher; printer markings: Made in U.S.A.; circa 1940s; no notice of copyright. $3.00 – 8.00.

Flat valentine; anonymous publisher; printer markings: Made in U.S.A.; circa 1940s; no notice of copyright. $3.00 – 8.00.

Chapter 20: 1940 – 1949 *Flat Cards*

Flat valentine; anonymous publisher; printer markings: Made in U.S.A.; circa 1940s; no notice of copyright. $3.00 – 8.00.

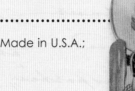

Flat valentine with easel; anonymous publisher; printer markings: Made in U.S.A.; circa 1940s; no notice of copyright. $3.00 – 8.00.

Flat valentine with easel; anonymous publisher; printer markings: Made in U.S.A.; circa 1940s; no notice of copyright. $3.00 – 8.00.

Flat valentine; anonymous publisher; printer markings: Made in U.S.A.; circa 1940s; no notice of copyright. $3.00 – 8.00.

Flat valentine with easel; anonymous publisher; printer markings: Made in U.S.A.; circa 1940s; no notice of copyright. $3.00 – 8.00.

Chapter 20: 1940 – 1949 Flat Cards

Flat valentine; anonymous publisher; printer markings: none; circa 1940s; no notice of copyright. $3.00 – 8.00.

Flat valentine with easel; anonymous publisher; printer markings: Made in U.S.A.; circa 1940s; no notice of copyright. $3.00 – 8.00.

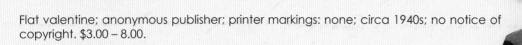

Flat valentine; anonymous publisher; printer markings: none; circa 1940s; no notice of copyright. $3.00 – 8.00.

Flat valentine; anonymous publisher; printer markings: Made in U.S.A.; circa 1940s; no notice of copyright. $3.00 – 8.00.

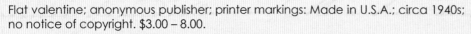

Flat valentine; anonymous publisher; printer markings: Made in U.S.A.; circa 1940s; no notice of copyright. $3.00 – 8.00.

Flat valentine; anonymous publisher; printer markings: Made in U.S.A.; circa 1940s; no notice of copyright. $3.00 – 8.00.

Flat valentine; anonymous publisher; printer markings: none; circa 1940s; no notice of copyright. $3.00 – 8.00.

Flat valentine; anonymous publisher; printer markings: Made in U.S.A.; circa 1940s; no notice of copyright. $3.00 – 8.00.

Flat valentine with easel; anonymous publisher; printer markings: Made in U.S.A.; circa 1940s; no notice of copyright. $3.00 – 8.00.

Flat valentine; anonymous publisher; printer markings: none; circa 1940s – 1950s; no notice of copyright. $3.00 – 8.00.

Flat valentine with easel; anonymous publisher; printer markings: Made in U.S.A.; circa 1940s; no notice of copyright. $3.00 – 8.00.

Flat valentine; anonymous publisher; printer markings: Made in U.S.A.; circa 1940s; no notice of copyright. $3.00 – 8.00.

Flat valentine; anonymous publisher; printer markings: none; circa 1940s; no notice of copyright. $10.00 – 15.00.

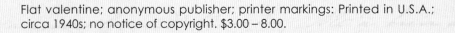

Flat valentine; anonymous publisher; printer markings: Printed in U.S.A.; circa 1940s; no notice of copyright. $3.00 – 8.00.

Flat valentine; anonymous publisher; printer markings: Made in U.S.A.; circa 1940s; no notice of copyright. $10.00 – 15.00.

Flat valentine; anonymous publisher; printer markings: Made in U.S.A.; circa 1940s; no notice of copyright. $3.00 – 8.00.

Flat valentine; anonymous publisher; printer markings: Made in U.S.A.; circa 1940s; no notice of copyright. $3.00 – 8.00.

Flat valentine; anonymous publisher; printer markings: Made in U.S.A.; circa 1940s; no notice of copyright. $3.00 – 8.00.

Flat valentine; anonymous publisher; printer markings: Made in U.S.A.; circa 1940s; no notice of copyright. $3.00 – 8.00.

Chapter 20: 1940 – 1949 *Flat Cards*

Flat valentine with easel; anonymous publisher; printer markings: Made in U.S.A.; circa 1940s; no notice of copyright. $3.00 – 8.00.

Flat valentine with easel; anonymous publisher; printer markings: Made in U.S.A.; circa 1940s; no notice of copyright. $3.00 – 8.00.

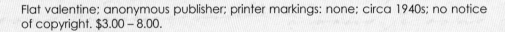

Flat valentine; anonymous publisher; printer markings: none; circa 1940s; no notice of copyright. $3.00 – 8.00.

Flat valentine with easel; anonymous publisher; printer markings: Made in U.S.A.; circa 1940s; no notice of copyright. $3.00 – 8.00.

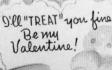

Flat valentine; anonymous publisher; printer markings: Made in U.S.A. circa 1940s – 1950s; no notice of copyright. $3.00 – 8.00.

Flat valentine with easel; anonymous publisher; printer markings: Made in U.S.A.; circa 1940s; no notice of copyright. $3.00 – 8.00.

Flat valentine with easel; anonymous publisher; printer markings: Made in U.S.A.; circa 1940s; no notice of copyright. $3.00 – 8.00.

Flat valentine with easel; anonymous publisher; printer markings: Made in U.S.A.; circa 1940s; no notice of copyright. $3.00 – 8.00.

Chapter 21
1940 ~ 1949
Fold Down & Novelty Cards

Fold down cards are the most clever innovations of the 1940s. Companies made small cards with fold down features showing a puff of honeycomb tissue paper. Some valentines had small fold out easels on the bottom sides of the cards. The most interesting type of fold down or fold out cards from the 1940s are those with small aspects of the design that fold out and extend beyond the original size of the card. Often showing motion or a hidden feature, these are the most entertaining of the decade's novelty valentines.

Anonymously Published Card
Markings Indicating Place of Manufacture or Printing

- Made in U.S.A

Types of Valentines Illustrated

- Cards with applied embellishments
- Cards with fold out features
- Fold down valentines
- Fold out valentines
- Pull out three-dimensional flower valentines

Design Features Illustrated

- Applied fabric swatches
- Metal embellishments
- Primary colors
- Side easels
- Thin cardboard paper

Subjects Illustrated

- Anthropomorphism
- Artists
- Aviators
- Bakers
- Bears
- Birds
- Cats
- Circus
- Couples
- Dogs
- Ethnic themes
- Female military members

- Flowers
- Hats that fold out
- Lions
- Military subjects
- Movie themes
- Objects that fold out
- Rabbits
- Radios
- Students
- Swimmers
- Sailors
- Teachers
- Telephones
- Transportation

Published Cards Not Illustrated

A.C. & Co Product of USA
- 1940 girl in blue bonnet with bluebird and fold out heart

Exact years in captions are original sender/receiver dates.

Fold out valentine; anonymous publisher; printer markings: Made in U.S.A.; circa 1940s; no notice of copyright. $5.00 – 7.00.

1944

Fold down valentine; anonymous publisher; printer markings: Made in U.S.A.; 1944; no notice of copyright. $7.00 – 13.00.

1945 – 1947

Fold out valentine; anonymous publisher; printer markings: Made in U.S.A.; circa 1945 – 1947; no notice of copyright. $10.00 – 15.00.

Fold out valentine; anonymous publisher; printer markings: Made in U.S.A.; circa 1945 – 1947; no notice of copyright. $7.00 – 13.00.

Fold out valentine; anonymous publisher; printer markings: Made in U.S.A.; circa 1945 – 1947; no notice of copyright. $7.00 – 13.00.

View of folded out pencil sharpener revealing a message.

Fold out valentine; anonymous publisher; printer markings: Made in U.S.A.; circa 1945 – 1947; no notice of copyright. $5.00 – 7.00.

Fold out valentine; anonymous publisher; printer markings: Made in U.S.A.; circa 1945 – 1947; no notice of copyright. $7.00 – 13.00.

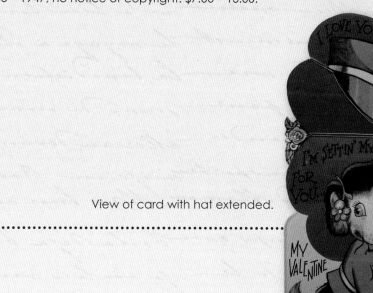

Fold out valentine; anonymous publisher; printer markings: Made in U.S.A.; circa 1945 – 1947; no notice of copyright. $7.00 – 13.00.

View of card with hat extended.

Fold out valentine; anonymous publisher; printer markings: Made in U.S.A.; circa 1945 – 1947; no notice of copyright. $7.00 – 13.00.

View of card with hat extended.

Fold out valentine; anonymous publisher; printer markings: Made in U.S.A.; circa 1945 – 1947; no notice of copyright. $7.00 – 13.00.

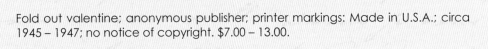

Fold out valentine; anonymous publisher; printer markings: Made in U.S.A.; circa 1945 – 1947; no notice of copyright. $7.00 – 13.00.

Fold out valentine; anonymous publisher; printer markings: Made in U.S.A.; circa 1945 – 1947; no notice of copyright. $7.00 – 13.00.

Fold out valentine; anonymous publisher; printer markings: Made in U.S.A.; circa 1945 – 1947; no notice of copyright. $7.00 – 13.00.

1946

Fold out valentine; anonymous publisher; printer markings: Made in U.S.A.; 1946; no notice of copyright. $5.00 – 7.00.

1948

Fold out valentine; anonymous publisher; printer markings: Made in U.S.A.; 1948; no notice of copyright. $5.00 – 7.00.

Applied fabric valentine; anonymous publisher; printer markings: Made in U.S.A.; circa 1930s – 1940s; no notice of copyright. $7.00 – 13.00.

Fold out valentine; anonymous publisher; printer markings: none; circa 1930s – 1940s; no notice of copyright. $5.00 – 7.00.

Applied metal embellishment valentine; anonymous publisher; printer markings: Made in U.S.A.; circa 1930s – 1940s; no notice of copyright. $7.00 – 13.00.

Pull out valentine; anonymous publisher; printer markings: Made in U.S.A.; circa 1930s – 1940s; no notice of copyright. $7.00 – 13.00.

Pull out valentine; anonymous publisher; printer markings: Made in U.S.A.; circa 1930s – 1940s; no notice of copyright. $7.00 – 13.00.

Pull out valentine; anonymous publisher; printer markings: Made in U.S.A.; circa 1930s – 1940s; no notice of copyright. $7.00 – 13.00.

Fold out valentine; anonymous publisher; printer markings: Made in U.S.A.; circa 1930s – 1940s; no notice of copyright. $5.00 – 7.00.

Fold out valentine; anonymous publisher; printer markings: none; circa 1940s; no notice of copyright. $7.00 – 13.00.

Applied foil decoration valentine; anonymous publisher; printer markings: Made in U.S.A.; circa 1930s – 1940s; no notice of copyright. $7.00 – 13.00.

Applied feather decoration; anonymous publisher; printer markings: Made in U.S.A.; circa 1940s; no notice of copyright. $7.00 – 13.00.

Fold out valentine; anonymous publisher; printer markings: Litho in U.S.A.; circa 1940s; no notice of copyright. $5.00 – 7.00.

1949

Fold out valentine; anonymous publisher; printer markings: Made in U.S.A.; 1949; no notice of copyright. $5.00 – 7.00.

Fold out valentine; anonymous publisher; printer markings: Made in U.S.A.; circa 1940s; no notice of copyright. $5.00 – 7.00.

Fold out valentine; anonymous publisher; printer markings: none; circa 1940s; no notice of copyright. $7.00 – 13.00.

View of card with hat extended.

Fold out valentine; anonymous publisher; printer markings: Made in U.S.A.; circa 1940s; no notice of copyright. $7.00 – 13.00.

View of card with girl extended.

Fold out valentine; anonymous publisher; printer markings: Made in U.S.A.; circa 1930s – 1940s; no notice of copyright. $5.00 – 7.00.

Fold out valentine; anonymous publisher; printer markings: Made in U.S.A.; circa 1940s; no notice of copyright. $7.00 – 13.00.

Fold out valentine; anonymous publisher; printer markings: Made in U.S.A.; circa 1940s; no notice of copyright. $7.00 – 13.00.

Fold out valentine; anonymous publisher; printer markings: Made in U.S.A.; circa 1940s; no notice of copyright. $7.00 – 13.00.

Fold out valentine; anonymous publisher; printer markings: Made in U.S.A.; circa 1940s; no notice of copyright. $7.00 – 13.00.

View of card with hat extended.

Fold out valentine; anonymous publisher; printer markings: Made in Canada; circa 1940s; no notice of copyright. $7.00 – 13.00.

Fold out valentine; anonymous publisher; printer markings: Made in Canada; circa 1940s; no notice of copyright. $7.00 – 13.00.

Fold out valentine; anonymous publisher; printer markings: none; circa 1940s; no notice of copyright. $5.00 – 7.00.

Fold out valentine; anonymous publisher; printer markings: Made in Canada; circa 1940s; no notice of copyright. $7.00 – 13.00.

Fold out valentine; anonymous publisher; printer markings: none; circa 1940s; no notice of copyright. $5.00 – 7.00.

Fold out valentine; anonymous publisher; printer markings: Made in U.S.A.; circa 1940s; no notice of copyright. $5.00 – 7.00.

Fold out valentine; anonymous publisher; printer markings: none; circa 1940s; no notice of copyright. $7.00 – 13.00.

Fold out valentine; anonymous publisher; printer markings: none; circa 1940s; no notice of copyright. $5.00 – 7.00.

Fold out valentine; anonymous publisher; printer markings: none; circa 1940s; no notice of copyright. $5.00 – 7.00.

Fold out valentine; anonymous publisher; printer markings: Made in U.S.A.; circa 1940s; no notice of copyright. $7.00 – 13.00.

Fold out valentine; anonymous publisher; printer markings: Made in U.S.A.; circa 1940s; no notice of copyright. $10.00 – 15.00.

Fold out valentine; anonymous publisher; printer markings: none; circa 1940s; no notice of copyright. $5.00 – 7.00.

Fold out valentine; anonymous publisher; printer markings: Made in U.S.A.; circa 1940s; no notice of copyright. $7.00 – 13.00.

Fold down valentine; anonymous publisher; printer markings: Made in U.S.A.; circa 1940s; no notice of copyright. $7.00 – 13.00.

Fold down valentine; anonymous publisher; printer markings: Made in U.S.A.; circa 1940s; no notice of copyright. $7.00 – 13.00.

Fold down valentine; anonymous publisher; printer markings: Made in U.S.A.; circa 1940s; no notice of copyright. $7.00 – 13.00.

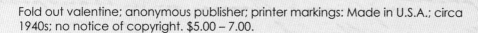

Fold out valentine; anonymous publisher; printer markings: Made in U.S.A.; circa 1940s; no notice of copyright. $5.00 – 7.00.

Chapter 22
1940 ~ 1949
Mechanical Cards

Mechanical valentines of the 1940s are distinctive by their style and artwork. These thin paper cards were simpler in their mechanical features than German mechanical cards of earlier decades. The paper and printing quality of 1940s cards is indicative of the shortages and restrictions of war. A single part accomplished movement thanks to a tiny rivet or flap. These delightful cards prove Americans never lost their love for motion and entertainment. Such novelty card themes illustrate what would concern or amuse young children. These cards reflect wartime patriotism, domestic themes, a fascination with animals, exotic characters, and innocent, childish experiences. Thematically, their message continues to relate love and affection. They are sweet and simplistic in their movement. These valentines echo a desire to maintain humor as America and the rest of the world faced loss and sacrifices during the war years.

Anonymously Published Card
Markings Indicating Place of Manufacture or Printing

- "Made in U.S.A."

Types of Valentines Illustrated

- Mechanical cards with riveted moving parts
- Small fold open elements

Design Features Illustrated

- Arms holding objects
- Bird wings that move
- Heads that pop up
- Moving eyes
- Moving limbs

Subjects Illustrated

- Airplanes
- Barnyard animals
- Birds
- Cars
- Cats
- Children
- Cinematic themes
- Circus animals
- Circus themes
- Cooking
- Cottages
- Couples
- Cows
- Dancing
- Dogs
- Domestic chores
- Domestic themes
- Ethnic themes
- Everyday pastimes
- Fans that move
- Firefighting
- Fishing
- Flags
- Food
- Gardening
- Kitchen items
- Military themes
- Nursery rhyme themes
- Owls
- Rabbits
- Riding horses
- Rowing
- Sailors
- Skiing
- Sledding
- Soldiers
- Sports
- Tanks
- Telephones
- Trains
- Zoo animals

Exact years in captions are original sender/receiver dates.

1941

Mechanical valentine, upper bodies of the girl and boy move; anonymous publisher; printer markings: U.S.A.; 1941; no notice of copyright. $7.00 – 13.00.

Mechanical valentine, zebra and rider move; anonymous publisher; printer markings: Made in U.S.A.; 1941; no notice of copyright. $7.00 – 13.00.

1942

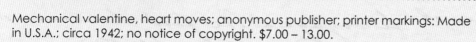

Mechanical valentine, eyes and upper body move; anonymous publisher; printer markings: Made in U.S.A.; circa 1942; no notice of copyright. $7.00 – 13.00.

Mechanical valentine, heart moves; anonymous publisher; printer markings: Made in U.S.A.; circa 1942; no notice of copyright. $7.00 – 13.00.

Mechanical valentine, figure moves; anonymous publisher; printer markings: Made in U.S.A.; circa 1942; no notice of copyright. $7.00 – 13.00.

Mechanical valentine, awning moves; anonymous publisher; printer markings: Made in U.S.A.; circa 1942; no notice of copyright. $7.00 – 13.00.

1943

Mechanical valentine, head moves; anonymous publisher; printer markings: none; 1943; no notice of copyright. $5.00 – 7.00.

1947

Mechanical valentine, wing moves; anonymous publisher; printer markings: Made in U.S.A.; circa 1947; no notice of copyright. $5.00 – 7.00.

1948

Mechanical, upper body moves; anonymous publisher; printer markings: Made in U.S.A.; 1948; no notice of copyright. $5.00 – 7.00.

Mechanical, sunshine moves; anonymous publisher; printer markings: Made in U.S.A.; 1948; no notice of copyright. $5.00 – 7.00.

Mechanical valentine, woman moves; anonymous publisher; printer markings: Made in U.S.A.; circa 1940s; no notice of copyright. $7.00 – 13.00.

Mechanical valentine, sailboat moves; anonymous publisher; printer markings: Made in U.S.A.; circa 1940s; no notice of copyright. $5.00 – 7.00.

Mechanical valentine, girl moves; anonymous publisher; printer markings: Made in U.S.A.; circa 1930s – 1940s; no notice of copyright. $5.00 – 7.00.

Mechanical valentine, boys move; anonymous publisher; printer markings: Made in U.S.A.; circa 1930s – 1940s; no notice of copyright. $5.00 – 7.00.

Mechanical valentine, boy moves; anonymous publisher; printer markings: Made in U.S.A.; circa 1940s; no notice of copyright. $10.00 – 15.00.

Chapter 22: 1940 - 1949 Mechanical Cards

Mechanical valentine, plane moves; anonymous publisher; printer markings: Made in U.S.A.; circa 1940s; no notice of copyright. $12.00 – 18.00.

Mechanical valentine, bears move; anonymous publisher; printer markings: Made in U.S.A.; circa 1930s – 1940s; no notice of copyright. $7.00 – 13.00.

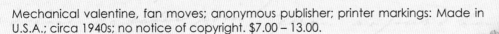

Mechanical valentine, fan moves; anonymous publisher; printer markings: Made in U.S.A.; circa 1940s; no notice of copyright. $7.00 – 13.00.

Mechanical valentine, cow and girl move; anonymous publisher; printer markings: Made in U.S.A.; circa 1940s; no notice of copyright. $7.00 – 13.00.

Mechanical valentine, owl head moves; anonymous publisher; printer markings: Made in U.S.A.; circa 1940s; no notice of copyright. $7.00 – 13.00.

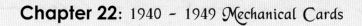

Mechanical valentine, arm moves; anonymous publisher; printer markings: none; circa 1940s; no notice of copyright. $10.00 – 18.00.

Mechanical valentine, legs and skis move; anonymous publisher; printer markings: Made in Canada; circa 1940s; no notice of copyright. $5.00 – 7.00.

Mechanical valentine, head moves; anonymous publisher; printer markings: Made in Canada; circa 1940s; no notice of copyright. $5.00 – 7.00.

Mechanical valentine, boy moves; anonymous publisher; printer markings: Made in U.S.A.; circa 1940s; no notice of copyright. $7.00 – 13.00.

Mechanical valentine, child moves; anonymous publisher; printer markings: Made in U.S.A.; circa 1940s; no notice of copyright. $7.00 – 13.00.

Mechanical valentine, cow moves; anonymous publisher; printer markings: Made in U.S.A.; circa 1940s; no notice of copyright. $7.00 – 13.00.

Mechanical valentine, arms and sled move; anonymous publisher; printer markings: Made in U.S.A.; circa 1940s; no notice of copyright. $7.00 – 13.00.

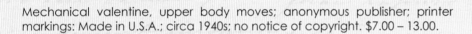

Mechanical valentine, upper body moves; anonymous publisher; printer markings: Made in U.S.A.; circa 1940s; no notice of copyright. $7.00 – 13.00.

Mechanical valentine, engineer moves; anonymous publisher: printer markings: Made in U.S.A.; circa 1940s; no notice of copyright. $7.00 – 13.00.

Mechanical valentine, film screen shots move; anonymous publisher; printer markings: Litho. in U.S.A.; circa 1940s; no notice of copyright. $7.00 – 13.00.

Mechanical valentine, girl moves; anonymous publisher; printer markings: Made in U.S.A.; circa 1940s; no notice of copyright. $7.00 – 13.00.

Mechanical valentine, girl's head moves; anonymous publisher; printer markings: Litho. in U.S.A.; circa 1940s; no notice of copyright. $7.00 – 13.00.

Mechanical valentine, girl moves; anonymous publisher; printer markings: Made in U.S.A.; circa 1940s; no notice of copyright. $7.00 – 13.00.

Mechanical valentine, girl's face moves; anonymous publisher; printer markings: Made in U.S.A.; circa 1940s; no notice of copyright. $7.00 – 13.00.

Mechanical valentine, girl moves; anonymous publisher; printer markings: Made in U.S.A.; circa 1940s; no notice of copyright. $7.00 – 13.00.

Mechanical valentine, phone dial moves; anonymous publisher; printer markings: Made in U.S.A.; circa 1940s; no notice of copyright. $7.00 – 13.00.

Mechanical valentine, couple moves; anonymous publisher; printer markings: Made in U.S.A.; circa 1940s; no notice of copyright. $5.00 – 7.00.

Mechanical valentine, girl moves; anonymous publisher; printer markings: Made in U.S.A.; circa 1930s – 1940s; no notice of copyright. $7.00 – 13.00.

Mechanical valentine, upper body of the man moves; anonymous publisher; printer markings: Made in U.S.A.; circa 1940s; no notice of copyright. $7.00 – 13.00.

Mechanical valentine, upper body of the bear moves; anonymous publisher; printer markings: Made in U.S.A.; circa 1940s; no notice of copyright. $7.00 – 13.00.

Mechanical valentine, arm moves; anonymous publisher; printer markings: Made in U.S.A.; circa 1940s; no notice of copyright. $7.00 – 13.00.

Mechanical valentine, cuckoo clock moves; anonymous publisher; printer markings: Made in U.S.A.; circa 1940s; no notice of copyright. $7.00 – 13.00.

Mechanical valentine, door moves; anonymous publisher; printer markings: Made in U.S.A.; circa 1940s; no notice of copyright. $7.00 – 13.00.

Mechanical valentine, boy moves; anonymous publisher; printer markings: Made in U.S.A.; circa 1940s; no notice of copyright. $8.00 – 14.00.

Mechanical valentine, legs move; anonymous publisher; printer markings: Made in U.S.A.; circa 1940s; no notice of copyright. $8.00 – 14.00.

Chapter 23
1900s – 1940s
Honeycomb Tissue
Paper Cards

Vibrant and novel, honeycomb tissue paper valentines have all the dramatic look of a party table centerpiece. Embellished with popular chromolithograph scraps, these valentines never cease to amaze collectors. Their bright colors and clever themes made them a sight to behold. It all began with the popular use of tissue paper during the early 1900s. Valentine makers learned to fashion tissue paper into a honeycomb shape that gave the card both a new three-dimensional shape and unique stand up decorative features. Taking hold from the 1900s through the 1930s, these cards have distinctive looks over the four decades of their existence. The earliest honeycomb tissue paper valentines date from the 1900s to 1910s. These were early three-dimensional cards created in Germany.[134] Their distinctive features include honeycomb tissue paper in different colors including blue, pink, and cream. Many of these cards were printed in Germany while other cards of these years bear no markings or indication of place of origin. Delightful chromolithograph scraps stand alongside the honeycomb tissue paper features. Subject matters include scraps of children which can assist us in dating by using styles of contemporary clothing from each of these decades.

Tissue paper provided valentine designers with the added dimension to fashion baskets, dangling torsos of figures, vases, birdcages, and even lighthouses. Publishers continued using creative elements including chromolithograph scraps around the honeycombs through the 1920s. Some German-made honeycomb valentines even featured wide, google-eyed children on their cards. Beistle of Shippensburg, Pennsylvania, is best known for making the large, lighter red shaped honeycomb tissue paper valentines of the 1920s and 1930s. During the late 1920s to the 1930s these lighter red tissue paper cards were also copied by other anonymous companies. Mimicking their designs, cards were produced featuring lighter red colored honeycombs with Art Deco-styled children, angels, floral design borders, and even the skirt of a female figure! Shortages during World War II more than likely prevented the further production of such cards. As one observes the changes in such cards from the late 1920s through the 1940s, tissue paper became less of a major design feature of American valentines. Instead forties cards used small amounts of tissue paper honeycombs as cleverly placed embellishments in the overall picture of the card's design. These clever bits of honeycomb became three-dimensional hearts, canopies, musical instruments, balls, furniture, hats, and umbrellas to name a few features.

Important Valentine Manufacturers, Publishers, and Printers

Beistle Company
- Beistle Company of Shippensburg, Pennsylvania, made honeycomb tissue paper valentines from the mid to late 1920s through the 1930s.

Anonymously Published Card
Markings Indicating Place of Manufacture or Printing

- "Germany"
- "Made in Germany"
- "Made in U.S.A."
- "Printed in Germany"

Types of Valentines Illustrated

- Honeycomb tissue paper accent valentines
- Honeycomb tissue paper valentines
- Three-dimensional valentines

Design Features Illustrated

- Chromolithograph scraps
- Honeycomb flower vases
- Honeycomb tissue paper ball accents

- Honeycomb tissue paper bases
- Honeycomb tissue paper baskets
- Honeycomb tissue paper bodies
- Honeycomb tissue paper dresses
- Honeycomb tissue paper furniture accents
- Honeycomb tissue paper hat accents
- Honeycomb tissue paper heart accents
- Honeycomb tissue paper hearts
- Honeycomb tissue paper lighthouses
- Honeycomb tissue paper mushroom-shaped bases
- Honeycomb tissue paper skirt accents
- Honeycomb tissue paper tops
- Honeycomb tissue paper umbrella accents
- Musical instrument honeycomb tissue paper accents

Subjects Illustrated

- Animals
- Baskets
- Birds
- Bowls
- Children
- Cupids
- Dresses
- Dutch children
- Flowers
- Forget-me-not flowers meaning: true love[135]
- Fountains
- Hearts
- Light houses
- Lily of the valley meaning in 1857: return of happiness[136]
- Nautical themes
- Roses meaning in 1857: beauty[137]

- Tulips meaning in 1857: a declaration of love[138]
- Vases
- Water pumps

Published Cards Not Illustrated

Beistle, Made in U.S.A. diamond shaped trademark
Cards have a value of $25.00 – 35.00 each.
- 1925 – 1927 cup-shaped red tissue paper, two cupids
- 1928 red tissue, cupid on the left, girl in lavender dress on the right, "Let our hearts with love combine then you will be my valentine," a large sized card

Beistle, Made in U.S.A. diamond shaped trademark
Cards have a value of $10.00 – 15.00 each. Beistle fans have a value of $30.00 – 50.00 each.
- 1930 cupids overlooking tissue cup, patent 159,3647, "A basket of love" (patents dated 1925 and 1926)
- 1931 red tissue paper wide top, column, and base, cupid with letter and box on the left, valentine greeting card on the right, small size
- 1920s – 1930s printed in U.S.A. tissue paper fan, "With all my love"
- 1920s – 1930s Cupid honeycomb fold down, "I send you the key to my heart," trademark Beistle
- 1920s – 1930s cupid's "Temple of Love" rotating a spinning wheel, red honeycomb tissue paper roof and base
- 1930s small floral tissue basket, "To my sweetheart"

Exact years in captions are original sender/receiver dates.

1900s – 1920s

Honeycomb tissue paper valentine; anonymous publisher; printer markings: Germany; circa 1900s – 1920s; no notice of copyright. $15.00 – 25.00.

Honeycomb tissue paper valentine; anonymous publisher; printer markings: Germany; circa 1910s – 1920s; no notice of copyright. $20.00 – 45.00.

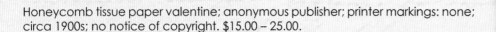

Honeycomb tissue paper valentine; anonymous publisher; printer markings: none; circa 1900s; no notice of copyright. $15.00 – 25.00.

Honeycomb tissue paper valentine; anonymous publisher; printer markings: none; circa 1910s – 1920s; no notice of copyright. $20.00 – 45.00.

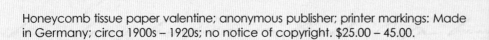

Honeycomb tissue paper valentine; anonymous publisher; printer markings: Made in Germany; circa 1900s – 1920s; no notice of copyright. $25.00 – 45.00.

Honeycomb tissue paper valentine; anonymous publisher; printer markings: none; circa 1900s – 1920s; no notice of copyright. $25.00 – 35.00.

Hanging or puppet valentine with honeycomb tissue paper body; anonymous publisher; printer markings: none; circa 1910s; no notice of copyright. $25.00 – 85.00.

Honeycomb tissue paper valentine; anonymous publisher; printer markings: none; circa 1900s – 1910s; no notice of copyright. $35.00 – 45.00.

Honeycomb tissue paper valentine; anonymous publisher; printer markings: none; circa 1900s – 1920s; no notice of copyright. $25.00 – 35.00.

Honeycomb tissue paper valentine; anonymous publisher; printer markings: none; circa 1900s – 1910s; no notice of copyright. $10.00 – 15.00.

Honeycomb tissue paper valentine; anonymous publisher; printer markings: none; circa 1900s – 1920s; no notice of copyright. $25.00 – 35.00.

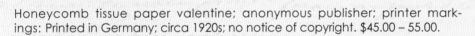

Honeycomb tissue paper valentine; anonymous publisher; printer markings: Printed in Germany; circa 1920s; no notice of copyright. $45.00 – 55.00.

Honeycomb tissue paper valentine; anonymous publisher; printer markings: none; circa 1900s – 1920s; no notice of copyright. $40.00 – 50.00.

Honeycomb tissue paper valentine; anonymous publisher; printer markings: Printed in Germany; circa 1920s; no notice of copyright. $45.00 – 55.00.

1928

Honeycomb tissue paper valentine; anonymous publisher; printer markings: Made in U.S.A.; 1928; no notice of copyright. $15.00 – 25.00.

1929

Honeycomb tissue paper valentine; anonymous publisher; printer markings: none; 1929; no notice of copyright. $25.00 – 45.00.

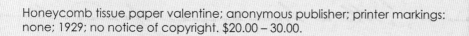

Honeycomb tissue paper valentine; anonymous publisher; printer markings: none; circa 1920s – 1930s; no notice of copyright. $20.00 – 30.00.

Honeycomb tissue paper valentine; anonymous publisher; printer markings: none; 1929; no notice of copyright. $20.00 – 30.00.

Honeycomb tissue paper valentine; anonymous publisher; printer markings: Made in U.S.A.; circa 1929; no notice of copyright. $20.00 – 30.00.

1920s – 1930s

Honeycomb tissue paper valentine; anonymous publisher; printer markings: none; circa 1920s – 1930s; no notice of copyright. $20.00 – 30.00.

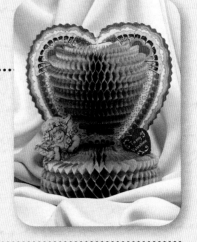

Honeycomb tissue paper valentine; anonymous publisher; printer markings: none; circa 1920s – 1930s; no notice of copyright. $15.00 – 20.00.

Honeycomb tissue paper valentine; anonymous publisher; printer markings: 10; circa 1920s – 1930s; no notice of copyright. $20.00 – 30.00.

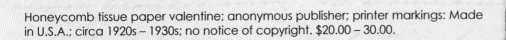

Honeycomb tissue paper valentine; anonymous publisher; printer markings: Made in U.S.A.; circa 1920s – 1930s; no notice of copyright. $20.00 – 30.00.

Honeycomb tissue paper valentine; anonymous publisher; printer markings: none; circa 1920s – 1930s; no notice of copyright. $15.00 – 20.00.

Honeycomb tissue paper valentine; anonymous publisher; printer markings: Made in U.S.A.; circa 1920s – 1930s; no notice of copyright. $20.00 – 30.00.

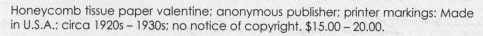

Honeycomb tissue paper valentine; anonymous publisher; printer markings: Made in U.S.A.; circa 1920s – 1930s; no notice of copyright. $15.00 – 20.00.

Honeycomb tissue paper valentine; anonymous publisher; printer markings: Made in U.S.A.; circa 1920s – 1930s; no notice of copyright. $15.00 – 20.00.

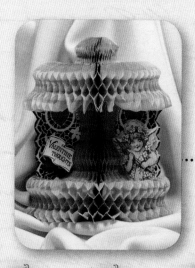

Honeycomb tissue paper valentine; anonymous publisher; printer markings: none; circa 1920s – 1930s; no notice of copyright. $15.00 – 20.00.

Honeycomb tissue paper valentine; anonymous publisher; printer markings: none; circa 1920s – 1930s; no notice of copyright. $20.00 – 30.00.

Honeycomb tissue paper valentine; anonymous publisher; printer markings: Made in U.S.A.; circa 1920s – 1930s; no notice of copyright. $15.00 – 20.00.

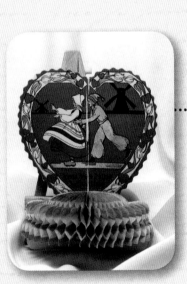

Honeycomb tissue paper valentine; anonymous publisher; printer markings: none; circa 1920s – 1930s; no notice of copyright. $20.00 – 30.00.

Honeycomb tissue paper valentine; anonymous publisher; printer markings: Made in U.S.AM.; circa 1920s – 1930s; no notice of copyright. $15.00 – 20.00.

Honeycomb tissue paper valentine; anonymous publisher; printer markings: Made in U.S.A.; circa 1920s – 1930s; no notice of copyright. $15.00 – 20.00.

Valentine with honeycomb tissue paper accent; anonymous publisher; printer markings: Made in Germany; circa 1920s – 1930s; no notice of copyright. $8.00 – 18.00.

Valentine with honeycomb tissue paper accent; anonymous publisher; printer markings: Printed in Germany; circa 1920s – 1930s; no notice of copyright. $8.00 – 18.00.

1931

Valentine with honeycomb tissue paper accent; anonymous publisher; printer markings: Printed in Germany; 1931; no notice of copyright. $8.00 – 18.00.

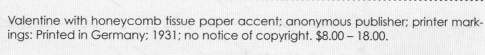

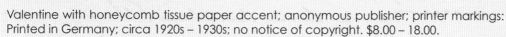

Valentine with honeycomb tissue paper accent; anonymous publisher; printer markings: Printed in Germany; circa 1920s – 1930s; no notice of copyright. $8.00 – 18.00.

Valentine with honeycomb tissue paper accent; anonymous publisher; printer markings: Germany; circa 1920s – 1930s; no notice of copyright. $8.00 – 18.00.

Valentine with honeycomb tissue paper accent; anonymous publisher; printer markings: Printed in Germany; circa 1920s – 1930s; no notice of copyright. $10.00 – 20.00.

1936

Valentine with honeycomb tissue paper accent; anonymous publisher; printer markings: none; circa 1936; no notice of copyright. $12.00 – 18.00.

Valentine with honeycomb tissue paper accent; anonymous publisher; printer markings: Printed in Germany; circa 1936; no notice of copyright. $12.00 – 18.00.

1938

Valentine with honeycomb tissue paper accent; anonymous publisher; printer markings: none; 1938; no notice of copyright. $8.00 – 18.00.

1930s ~ 1940s

Valentine with honeycomb tissue paper accent; anonymous publisher; printer markings: Made in U.S.A.; circa late 1930s – 1940s; no notice of copyright. $8.00 – 18.00.

1942

Valentine with honeycomb tissue paper accent; anonymous publisher; printer markings: Made in U.S.A.; 1942; no notice of copyright. $8.00 – 18.00.

Valentine with honeycomb tissue paper accent; anonymous publisher; printer markings: none; circa 1940s; no notice of copyright. $8.00 – 18.00.

Valentine with honeycomb tissue paper accent; anonymous publisher; printer markings: Made in Canada; circa 1940s; no notice of copyright. $8.00 – 18.00.

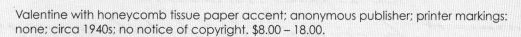

Valentine with honeycomb tissue paper accent; anonymous publisher; printer markings: none; circa 1940s; no notice of copyright. $8.00 – 18.00.

Valentine with honeycomb tissue paper accent; anonymous publisher; printer markings: none; circa 1940s; no notice of copyright. $8.00 – 18.00.

Valentine with honeycomb tissue paper accent; anonymous publisher; printer markings: Made in U.S.A.; circa 1940s; no notice of copyright. $8.00 – 18.00.

Valentine with honeycomb tissue paper accent; anonymous publisher; printer markings: Made in U.S.A.; circa 1930s – 1940s; no notice of copyright. $8.00 – 18.00.

Valentine with honeycomb tissue paper accent; anonymous publisher; printer markings: Made in U.S.A.; circa 1940s; no notice of copyright. $8.00 – 18.00.

Valentine with honeycomb tissue paper accent; anonymous publisher; printer markings: Made in U.S.A.; circa 1940s; no notice of copyright. $8.00 – 18.00.

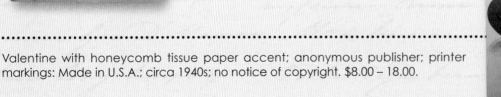

Valentine with honeycomb tissue paper accent; anonymous publisher; printer markings: Made in U.S.A.; circa 1940s; no notice of copyright. $8.00 – 18.00.

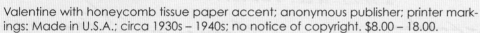

Valentine with honeycomb tissue paper accent; anonymous publisher; printer markings: Made in U.S.A.; circa late 1930s – 1940s; no notice of copyright. $8.00 – 18.00.

Valentine with honeycomb tissue paper accent; anonymous publisher; printer markings: Made in U.S.A.; circa 1930s – 1940s; no notice of copyright. $8.00 – 18.00.

Valentine with honeycomb tissue paper accent; anonymous publisher; printer markings: none; circa 1940s; no notice of copyright. $8.00 – 18.00.

1949

Valentine with honeycomb tissue paper accent; anonymous publisher; printer markings: Made in U.S.A.; 1949; no notice of copyright. $8.00 – 18.00.

Valentine with honeycomb tissue paper accent; anonymous publisher; printer markings: Made in U.S.A.; 1949; no notice of copyright. $8.00 – 18.00.

Chapter 24
18th Century – 1950s
Vinegar Valentines

Vinegar valentines began in the eighteenth century and enjoyed prolific popularity to the 1950s. Vinegar valentines were woodcuts with verses printed on cheap paper done in poor quality print.[139] Engravings caricaturing men and women poked fun at false pride, bad looks, the down side to job professions, and every negative aspect of human behavior. These valentines joked at or ridiculed the poor recipient giving the sender a caustic weapon and an annual opportunity to say what he or she "truly thought" but never dared to say every other day of the year. They were rarely signed but instances do survive here and there. Whether mocking the recipient's failings, flaws, or negative personality features they became the source of misery during a holiday devoted to romance and love. These cards are the antithesis of the sentimental valentine. Their popularity shows people loved to make fun of one another as well as fall in love or show affection.

Important Valentine Manufacturers, Publishers, and Printers

18th Century to the 1830s
English comic valentines remained popular from the eighteenth century to the 1830s. Their themes poked fun at old maids and vulgar men. These rude cards grew out of a tradition of early caricatures similar to the engravings of William Hogarth, Thomas Rowlandson, and George and Robert Cruikshank. Publishers of early comics during these decades included Park, Dobbs and Kidd, Alfred Henry Forrester (Alfred Crowquill drew comics 1830s to 1840s), Elton and Company, A.J. Fisher, and Robert H. Elton of New York (1833).[140]

1840s
Comic valentines became even more popular during the 1840s. Hand-colored wood block comics were inexpensive and simple to reproduce. Important comic valentine makers during the 1840s included A.J. Fisher, J.L. Marks, J.T. Wood, J & F Harwood (drew ladies with parrot heads), A. Park of London (drew men with insect bodies), W.S. Fortey, Alfred Henry Forrester (Alfred Crowquill), Charles P. Huestis (1842 – 1853), Turner & Fisher (1847), T. Frere, Jonathan King, Sr. (1845), Thomas W. Strong (1842 onwards), McLoughlin Brothers, and James Wrigley (1846 – 1870). Political subjects and intemperance were two poplar themes of comics during this decade.[141]

1850s
Valentine senders continued to perpetuate the custom of mixing comedy with romance during St. Valentine's Day. During the 1850s people sent joke parcels to rivals or mock postage due letters. Comic valentine makers included Turner & Fisher, Jonathan King, Sr., C. Huestis of New York, Lloyd of Fleet Street, Charles Magnus (1854 – 1870), and Elliot, Maurice & Company. Dean and Company made mechanical comic valentines at this time. T. Frere designed comics that featured themes regarding intemperance (1852 – 1855). Valentines showing men with insect bodies and ladies with parrot heads drawn by Park and Harwood continued through this decade. Comics in the 1850s poked fun at trades.[142]

1860s
Important mid-nineteenth century comic valentine makers included Rock & Company, Pickering & Company, R. Carr, G. Gilbert, Elliot, G. Ingram, E. Lloyd, J. Simmons & Company, and George Dunn & Company (1864). The New York Union Valentine Company featured valentines with military and Civil War themes.[143]

1870s – Late Victorian
Comic valentines achieved through cheap colored printing continued to be printed in English in the 1870s onward.[144]

McLoughlin Brothers of New York
McLoughlin Brothers of New York made wood blocked comic valentines. Most McLoughlin stock was damaged in a flood in Springfield, Massachusetts. Charles Howard designed comic valentines for McLoughlin Brothers. His tell-tale signature is an "H." George Whitney hated these cards so much it was rumored he bought out two rival companies in the 1870s because the other companies distributed the comic valentines he hated.[145]

Types of Valentines Illustrated

- Comics
- Paper sheets
- Penny dreadfuls
- Penny sours
- Postcards
- Slams[146]
- Vinegar valentines

Design Features Illustrated

- Crude printing
- Early hand-painted features
- Primary colors
- Thin paper
- Two-tone colors

Subjects Illustrated

- Caricatures
- Female foibles
- Female insecurities
- Good natured jokes[147]
- Insulting remarks
- Lampooning professions
- Male foibles
- Male insecurities
- Twists of words[148]

Published Cards Not Illustrated

E. Weaver Signature, Comic Valentine
- 1910s – 1920s "To the Artist," painted character

Exact years in captions are original sender/receiver dates.

Vinegar valentine; anonymous publisher; printer markings: signed "H" for Charles J. Howard; circa 1890s – 1900s; no notice of copyright. $15.00 – 20.00.

Vinegar valentine; anonymous publisher; printer markings: signed "H" for Charles J. Howard; original design from the 1890s – 1900s, subsequent reprinted marked: Printed in U.S.AM.; no notice of copyright. $15.00 – 20.00.

Vinegar valentine; anonymous publisher; printer markings: signed "H" for Charles J. Howard; circa 1900s; no notice of copyright. $15.00 – 20.00.

Vinegar valentine; anonymous publisher; printer markings: signed "H" for Charles J. Howard; original design circa 1900s, subsequent reprint marked: Printed in U.S.AM.; no notice of copyright. $15.00 – 20.00.

Vinegar valentine; anonymous publisher; printer markings: signed "H" for Charles J. Howard; circa 1890s – 1900s; no notice of copyright. $20.00 – 30.00.

Vinegar valentine; anonymous publisher; printer markings: none; original design from the 1900s, subsequent reprint marked: Printed in U.S.AM.; no notice of copyright. $10.00 – 20.00.

1900s

Vinegar valentine; anonymous publisher; printer markings: signed "H" for Charles J. Howard; circa 1900s; no notice of copyright. $15.00 – 20.00.

Vinegar valentine; anonymous publisher; printer markings: signed "H" for Charles J. Howard; circa 1900s; no notice of copyright. $15.00 – 20.00.

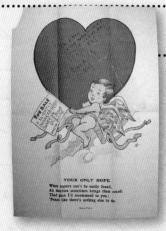

Vinegar valentine; anonymous publisher; printer markings: signed "H" for Charles J. Howard; original design from the 1900s, subsequent reprint marked: Made in U.S.A.; no notice of copyright. $15.00 – 20.00.

Vinegar valentine; anonymous publisher; printer markings: signed "H" for Charles J. Howard; original design from the 1900s, subsequent reprint marked: Made in U.S.A.; no notice of copyright. $15.00 – 20.00.

Vinegar valentine; anonymous publisher; printer markings: signed "H" for Charles J. Howard; original design from the 1900s, subsequent reprint marked: Printed in U.S. AM.; no notice of copyright. $10.00 – 15.00.

Vinegar valentine; anonymous publisher; printer markings: signed "H" for Charles J. Howard; circa 1900s; no notice of copyright. $10.00 – 15.00.

Vinegar valentine; anonymous publisher; printer markings: signed "H" for Charles J. Howard; circa 1900s; no notice of copyright. $10.00 – 15.00.

Vinegar valentine; anonymous publisher; printer markings: signed "H" for Charles J. Howard; circa 1900s; no notice of copyright. $10.00 – 15.00.

Vinegar valentine; anonymous publisher; printer markings: none; original design from the 1900s – 1910s, subsequent reprint marked: Printed in U.S.AM.; no notice of copyright. $10.00 – 20.00.

Vinegar valentine; anonymous publisher; printer markings: none; original design from the 1900s – 1910s, subsequent reprinted marked: Printed in U.S.AM.; no notice of copyright. $10.00 – 20.00.

Vinegar valentine; anonymous publisher; printer markings: "H" for Charles Howard; original design from the 1900s – 1910s, subsequent reprint marked: Printed in U.S.AM.; no notice of copyright. $10.00 – 20.00.

Postcard of a vinegar valentine; anonymous publisher; printer markings: none; circa 1900s; no notice of copyright. $5.00 – 15.00.

1908

Postcard of a vinegar valentine; anonymous publisher; printer markings: none; postmark February 14; 1908; no notice of copyright. $5.00 – 15.00.

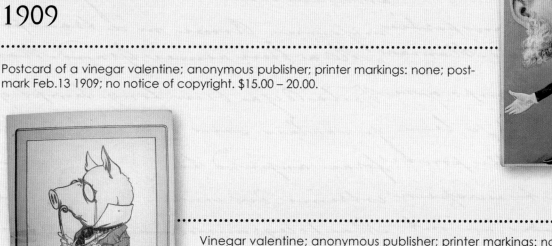

1909

Postcard of a vinegar valentine; anonymous publisher; printer markings: none; postmark Feb.13 1909; no notice of copyright. $15.00 – 20.00.

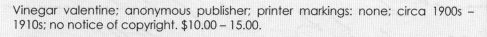

Vinegar valentine; anonymous publisher; printer markings: none; circa 1900s – 1910s; no notice of copyright. $10.00 – 15.00.

Vinegar valentine; anonymous publisher; printer markings: none; circa 1900s – 1910s; no notice of copyright. $10.00 – 15.00.

Vinegar valentine; anonymous publisher; printer markings: none; circa 1900s – 1910s; no notice of copyright. $10.00 – 15.00.

Vinegar valentine; anonymous publisher; printer markings: none; original design from the 1900s – 1910s, subsequent reprint marked: Printed in U.S.AM.; no notice of copyright. $10.00 – 15.00.

Vinegar valentine; anonymous publisher; printer markings: none; circa 1900s – 1910s; no notice of copyright. $10.00 – 15.00.

Vinegar valentine; anonymous publisher; printer markings: none; original design from the 1900s – 1910s, subsequent reprint marked: Printed in U.S.AM.; no notice of copyright. $10.00 – 15.00.

1910s

Vinegar valentine; anonymous publisher; printer markings: signed "H" for Charles J. Howard; circa 1910s; no notice of copyright. $10.00 – 15.00.

Vinegar valentine; anonymous publisher; printer markings: none; circa 1910s; no notice of copyright. $10.00 – 15.00.

Vinegar valentine; anonymous publisher; printer markings: none; circa 1910s; no notice of copyright. $10.00 – 15.00.

Vinegar valentine; anonymous publisher; printer markings: none; circa 1910s; no notice of copyright. 10.00 – 15.00.

Vinegar valentine; anonymous publisher; printer markings: none; circa 1910s; no notice of copyright. $10.00 – 15.00.

Vinegar valentine; anonymous publisher; printer markings: none; circa 1910s; no notice of copyright. $10.00 – 15.00.

Vinegar valentine; anonymous publisher; printer markings: none; circa 1910s; no notice of copyright. $10.00 – 15.00.

Vinegar valentine; anonymous publisher; printer markings: signed "H" for Charles J. Howard; circa 1910s; no notice of copyright. $10.00 – 15.00.

Postcard of a vinegar valentine; anonymous publisher; printer markings: none; circa 1910s; no notice of copyright. $5.00 – 15.00.

Vinegar valentine; anonymous publisher; printer markings: Printed in Germany; circa 1910s – 1920s; no notice of copyright. $15.00 – 20.00.

1920s

Vinegar valentine; anonymous publisher; printer markings: none; circa late 1920s – early 1930s; no notice of copyright. $10.00 – 15.00.

Vinegar valentine; anonymous publisher; printer markings: none; circa late 1920s – early 1930s; no notice of copyright. $10.00 – 15.00.

Vinegar valentine; anonymous publisher; printer markings: Printed in U.S.AM.; circa late 1920s – early 1930s; no notice of copyright. $6.00 – 9.00.

1930s

Vinegar valentine; anonymous publisher; printer markings: Made in U.S.A.; circa 1930s; no notice of copyright. $10.00 – 15.00.

Vinegar valentine; anonymous publisher; printer markings: Made in U.S.A.; circa 1930s; no notice of copyright. $10.00 – 15.00.

1939

Vinegar valentine; anonymous publisher; printer markings: Printed in U.S. AM.; circa 1939; no notice of copyright. $10.00 – 15.00.

1930s – 1940s

Vinegar valentine; anonymous publisher; printer markings: Printed in U.S.A.; circa 1930s – 1940s; no notice of copyright. $5.00 – 10.00.

Vinegar valentine; anonymous publisher; printer markings: Printed in U.S.A.; circa 1930s – 1940s; no notice of copyright. $5.00 – 10.00.

Vinegar valentine; anonymous publisher; printer markings: none; circa 1930s – 1940s; no notice of copyright. $5.00 – 10.00.

Vinegar valentine; anonymous publisher; printer markings: Printed in U.S.A.; circa 1930s – 1940s; no notice of copyright. $5.00 – 10.00.

1940s

Vinegar valentine; anonymous publisher; printer markings: Made in U.S.A.; circa 1940s; no notice of copyright. $5.00 – 10.00.

1943

Vinegar valentine; anonymous publisher; printer markings: Made in U.S.A.; 1943; no notice of copyright. $5.00 – 10.00.

1944

Vinegar valentine; anonymous publisher; printer markings: Made in U.S.A.; 1944; no notice of copyright. $5.00 – 10.00.

1947

Vinegar valentine; anonymous publisher; printer markings: Made in U.S.A.; 1947; no notice of copyright. $5.00 – 10.00.

1940s – 1950s

Vinegar valentine; anonymous publisher; printer markings: none; circa 1940s – 1950s; no notice of copyright. $5.00 – 10.00.

Vinegar valentine; anonymous publisher; printer markings: none; circa 1940s – 1950s; no notice of copyright. $5.00 – 10.00.

Vinegar valentine; anonymous publisher; printer markings: none; circa 1940s – 1950s; no notice of copyright. $5.00 – 10.00.

Vinegar valentine; anonymous publisher; printer markings: none; circa 1940s – 1950s; no notice of copyright. $5.00 – 10.00.

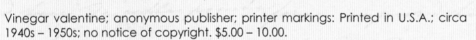

Vinegar valentine; anonymous publisher; printer markings: none; circa 1940s – 1950s; no notice of copyright. $5.00 – 10.00.

Vinegar valentine; anonymous publisher; printer markings: Printed in U.S.A.; circa 1940s – 1950s; no notice of copyright. $5.00 – 10.00.

1950s

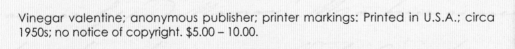

Vinegar valentine; anonymous publisher; printer markings: Printed in U.S.A.; circa 1950s; no notice of copyright. $5.00 – 10.00.

Vinegar valentine; anonymous publisher; printer markings: Printed in U.S.A.; circa 1950s; no notice of copyright. $5.00 – 10.00.

Chapter 25
1950 ~ 1959
Flat Cards

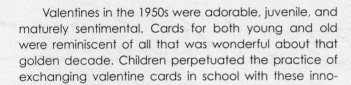

Valentines in the 1950s were adorable, juvenile, and maturely sentimental. Cards for both young and old were reminiscent of all that was wonderful about that golden decade. Children perpetuated the practice of exchanging valentine cards in school with these inno- cent and adorable images. Cards radiate 1950s lettering styles and artistic designs. American greeting card man- ufacturers took advantage of the prosperity after World War II to continue to market to the public delightful cards in the hopes of being popular to children and adults.

Published Cards Not Illustrated

Ambassador Cards, Made in USA
Cards are $3.00 – 8.00 each.
- 1950s fold down, gondolier, couple, roses, cupids, "To the one I love," Made in USA

American Greetings, Cleveland, Ohio
Cards are $3.00 – 8.00 each.
- 1950s bear, slate, "For Teacher"
- 1950s duck with eyelashes
- 1950s – early 1960s cat, teacher card
- 1950s – early 1960s farm couple pulling weeds
- 1950s – early 1960s fold down, man and woman on carousel

Americard
Cards are $3.00 – 8.00 each.
- 1950s girl fold out, teacher, globe

Cut-out or Punch-out Cards from Unknown Published Booklets
Cards are $3.00 – 8.00.
- 1950s angry dog in dog house, "Dog-gone it, I wan- na be your valentine"
- 1950s die-cut dog, postman with large valentine letter
- 1950s dog mailing heart in mail box, inserted valen- tine letter
- 1950s easel style heart with dog and inserted valen- tine letter, side points to fold back
- 1950s fold open card, bear with heart on left side when opened
- 1950s fold open card, gray bunny holding a heart
- 1950s fold open card with bunny, heart, and blue- bird on branch
- 1950s fold open card, girl with tilted head
- 1950s heart-shaped card with elephant, "The big- gest heart is for you"
- 1950s heart-shaped die-cut of bluebird delivering gold open "For you" message
- 1950s kitten holding heart, "To the sweetest one of all"
- 1950s two deer, "You are a little dear, will you be my valentine?" fold open card
- 1950s two gray kittens with heart

Forget Me Not Card, Cleveland, Ohio (O in Circle)
Cards are $3.00 – 8.00 each.
- 1950s girl in old-fashioned dress mailing letter
- 1950s peacock and pear couple
- 1950s pirate teacher valentine
- 1950s black puppy, copper foil heart, for teacher

Hallmark
Cards are $3.00 – 8.00 each.
- 1950s frog with flies
- 1950s roses
- 1950s – early 1960s bunny and teacher
- 1950s – early 1960s glitter card
- 1963 two dogs and heart

Rust Craft, Boston
Cards have a value of $9.00 – 17.00 each.
- 1950s girl knitting heart, easel, and brushes
- 1951 bunny, heart, teacher valentine

Whitman, Made in USA
Cards are $3.00 – 8.00 each.
- 1950s dog in bonnet, teacher card
- 1950s dog and boy holding gift
- 1950s puppy and kitten in basket, teacher card
- 1950s flocked red pony, teacher valentine

Exact years in captions are original sender/receiver dates.

Flat valentine; anonymous publisher; printer markings: Made in U.S.A.; circa 1950s; no notice of copyright. $3.00 – 8.00.

Flat valentine; anonymous publisher; printer markings: Made in U.S.A.; circa 1950s; no notice of copyright. $3.00 – 8.00.

Flat valentine; anonymous publisher; printer markings: none; circa 1950s; no notice of copyright. $3.00 – 8.00.

1951

Flat valentine; anonymous publisher; printer markings: Made in U.S.A.; 1951; no notice of copyright. $3.00 – 8.00.

Flat valentine; anonymous publisher; printer markings: none; circa 1950s; no notice of copyright. $3.00 – 8.00.

Flat valentine; anonymous publisher; printer markings: Made in U.S.A.; circa 1950s; no notice of copyright. $3.00 – 8.00.

Flat valentine; anonymous publisher; printer markings: Made in U.S.A.; circa 1950s; no notice of copyright. $3.00 – 8.00.

1954

Flat valentine; anonymous publisher; printer markings: Made in U.S.A.; 1954; no notice of copyright. $3.00 – 8.00.

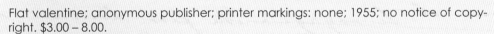

1955

Flat valentine; anonymous publisher; printer markings: none; 1955; no notice of copyright. $3.00 – 8.00.

Flat valentine; anonymous publisher; printer markings: Made in U.S.A.; circa 1950s; no notice of copyright. $3.00 – 8.00.

Flat valentine; anonymous publisher; printer markings: Made in U.S.A.; circa 1950s; no notice of copyright. $3.00 – 8.00.

1958 – 1959

Flat valentine; anonymous publisher; printer markings: Made in U.S.A.; circa 1958 – 1959; no notice of copyright. $5.00 – 10.00.

Flat valentine; anonymous publisher; printer markings: none; circa 1950s; no notice of copyright. $3.00 – 8.00.

Flat valentine; anonymous publisher; printer markings: Made in U.S.A.; circa 1950s; no notice of copyright. $3.00 – 8.00.

Chapter 26
1950 – 1959
Mechanical Cards

America enjoyed a decade of peace and prosperity after the second World War. American school children continued to follow the practice of valentine card exchanges. Children continued their fascination with mechanical cards. Popular for decades, the mechanical valentine was favored and fashionable in the 1950s. Popular American themes were abundant. America's youth found fascination with the exotic as well as the ordinary. The nature of the valentine's artwork is reflective of 1950s tastes and cartoon designs. Some adorable anonymous cards continued to be produced. American styles adopted new ideas rather than cling to old-fashioned valentine subjects.

Subjects Illustrated

- Birds
- Boys
- Cats
- Dogs
- Ethnic
- Girls
- Indians

Exact years in captions are original sender/receiver dates.

1951

Mechanical valentine, hat and eyes move; anonymous publisher; printer markings: none; 1951; no notice of copyright. $3.00 – 8.00.

Mechanical valentine, lower body and legs move; anonymous publisher; printer markings: Made in U.S.A.; circa 1950s; no notice of copyright. $6.00 – 12.00.

Mechanical valentine, head moves; anonymous publisher; printer markings: Litho. in U.S.A.; circa 1950s; no notice of copyright. $6.00 – 12.00.

Mechanical valentine, upper body moves; anonymous publisher; printer markings: none; circa 1950s; no notice of copyright. $3.00 – 8.00.

Mechanical valentine, upper body moves; anonymous publisher; printer markings: Litho. in U.S.A.; circa 1950s; no notice of copyright. $3.00 – 8.00.

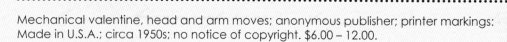

Mechanical valentine, head and arm moves; anonymous publisher; printer markings: Made in U.S.A.; circa 1950s; no notice of copyright. $6.00 – 12.00.

Mechanical valentine, head moves; anonymous publisher; printer markings: Made in U.S.A.; circa 1950s; no notice of copyright. $6.00 – 12.00.

Mechanical valentine, head moves; anonymous publisher; printer markings: none; circa 1950s; no notice of copyright. $6.00 – 12.00.

Endnotes

1   *Harper's Weekly, A Journal of Civilization*, New York, Saturday, February 13, 1858, Vol. II – No. 59, p. 104.
2   George Buday, *A History of the Christmas Card*, London: Spring Books, 1954. p. 262; Frank Staff, *The Valentine & Its Origins*, New York & Washington: Frederick A Praeger Inc. Publishers, 1969, pp. 42, 72.
3   Alistair Allen and Joan Hoverstadt, *The History of Printed Scraps*, London: New Cavendish Books, 1983, p. 9.
4   Buday, p. 267; Lou W. McCulloch, *Paper Americana: A Collector's Guide*, San Diego & New York: A.S. Baines & Co., Inc. also published by London: The Tantivy Press, 1980, p. 167; Staff, pp. 41 – 42.
5   Allen, p. 136.
6   Allen, p. 146.
7   Buday, p. 282; McCulloch, p. 171; Staff, p. 72; Ruth Webb Lee, *A History of Valentines*, Wellesley Hills, Massachusetts: Lee Publications, the Studio Publications Inc., 5th edition, 1952, p. 181.
8   Buday, p. 266; Allen, p. 134; Staff, p. 77; Lee, p. 174.
9   Lee, p. 40.
10 Lee, pp. 39 – 40.
11 Buday, p. 275; Staff, p. 72; Allen, p. 146.
12 Lee, p. 39.
13 Mrs. Willoughby Hodgson, "Valentines" *The Magazine Antiques*, February, 1930, Vol. XVI, No. 2, pp. 146 – 147.
14 Lee, pp. 8 – 11, 16, 20, 23, 26; Staff, pp. 26 – 29, 30, 32, 37, 41, 51 – 54.
15 Marsh, p. 50.
16 Catherine Waterman, b. 1812. *Flora's Lexicon, an interpretation of the language and sentiment of flowers: with an outline of botany and a poetical introduction*, Boston: Phillips, Sampson, and Company. New York: J.C. Derby, 1857, p. 246.
17 Jean Marsh, *The Illuminated Language of Flowers*, New York: Holt, Rinehart and Winston, 1978, p. 40.
18 Ernest Dudley Chase, *The Romance of Greeting Cards*, Cambridge Massachusetts: University Press, 1926, p. 64, second color insert page.
19 Waterman, p. 248.
20 Lee, p. 17, 20, 33; Staff, p. 32, 53.
21 Buday, p. 267; McCulloch, p. 167.
22 Staff, p. 62; Lee, p. 40.
23 Lee, pp. 39 – 40.
24 Lee, pp. 51 – 54; Staff, pp. 92 – 93.
25 Lee, pp. 43 – 45.
26 Buday, p. 272; Staff, p. 73.
27 Buday, p. 272; Allen, p. 143; Staff, pp. 85 – 87.
28 McCulloch, p. 169.
29 McCulloch, p. 169; Allen, p. 146; Buday, p. 275.
30 McCulloch, p. 169; Staff p. 72; Buday, p. 275.
31 Lee, p. 45.

34 McCulloch, p. 169; Buday, p. 276.
35 Staff, p.72
36 McCulloch, p. 170; Lee, p. 41.
37 Lee, p. 39.
38 Lee, p. 181; Staff, p. 72.
39 McCulloch, p. 171; Allen, p. 156.
40 Staff, pp. 56 – 57, 77, 79 – 80; Lee, pp. 32, 39 – 43.
41 Staff, pp. 56 – 57, 62, 72, 81; Lee, pp. 32, 36, 39 – 44; Chase, p. 65.
42 Lee, pp. 33 – 34; Staff, pp. 53, 56 – 57, 58 – 60, 62, 72 – 73, 85 – 87.
43 Staff, pp. 62 – 63; 81; Lee, pp. 42 – 43, 133, 137, 166 – 167.
44 Lee, pp. 39; 43; Staff, p. 78.
45 *Harper's, Weekly*, February 13, 1858, p. 105.
46 *Harper's, Weekly*, February 13, 1858, pp. 104 – 105.
47 Buday, p. 267; McCulloch, p. 166.
48 Lee, pp. 39 – 40.
49 Buday, p. 272; Allen, p. 143; Staff, p. 87.
50 McCulloch, p. 169; Patricia Fenn and Alfred P. Malpa, *Rewards of Merit*, The Ephemera Society of America, Charlottesville, Virgina: Howell Press, 1994, p. 209.
51 Buday, p. 278; Lee, pp. 47 – 48.
52 Allen, p. 150; Staff, p. 77; Buday, p. 279.
53 Buday, p. 282; Lee, p. 67; Staff, p. 97.
54 Lee, p. 181; Staff, p. 72.
55 Lee, pp. 39; 43 – 46; Staff, p. 79.
56 Staff, pp. 78, 104; Lee, pp. 43, 151, 167; *Harper's Weekly*, p. 105.
57 Staff, p. 67.
58 Waterman, p. 247, Staff, p. 67.
59 *Harper's Weekly*, p. 105; Staff, p. 73.
60 Mrs. Willoughby Hodgson, "Valentines" *The Magazine Antiques*, February, 1930, Vol. XVI, No. 2, p. 149.
61 Buday, p. 269; McCulloch, p. 168.
62 Buday, p. 269; Allen, p. 138; Staff p. 79.
63 Staff, pp. 92 – 94; Lee, pp. 51, 60.
64 Buday, p. 272; Staff, pp. 86 – 88.
65 Staff, p. 103.
66 Buday, p. 278; Allen, p. 148; Lee, p. 47.
67 Buday, p. 278; Staff, p. 100; McCulloch, p. 170; Lee, p. 190.
68 Buday, p. 280; Staff, p. 100.
69 Buday, p. 281; Fenn and Malpa, p. 213; Pamela E., Apkarian-Russell, *Postmarked Yesterday: Art of the Holiday Postcard*, Portland, Oregon: Collector's Press, 2001, p. 19; Allen, p. 154.
70 Buday, p. 281; McCulloch, p. 171; Staff, pp. 105 – 106; Allen, p. 155.
71 Buday, p. 282; McCulloch, p. 171; Apkarian-Russell, p. 18; Staff p. 97; Lee pp. 67 – 68, 71.
72 Lee, pp. 47 – 49, 68; Staff, pp. 104 – 105.

Endnotes

74 Lee, pp. 47 – 49, 68; Staff, pp. 104 – 105.

75 Lee, pp. 60, 64; Staff, p. 97.

76 McCulloch, p. 169; Michele Karl, *Greetings with Love, The Book of Valentines*, Gretna, Louisiana, Pelican Publishing Co., Inc, 2003, p. 24.

77 McCulloch, p. 169; Fenn and Malpa, p. 209.

78 Buday, p. 278; Alistair Allen, p. 149; Lee, pp. 47 – 48.

79 Buday, p. 278; Staff, p. 79.

80 Lee, pp. 63 – 64; McCulloch, p. 170.

81 Buday, p. 281; Fenn and Malpa, p. 213; Apkarian-Russell, p 19; Allen, p. 154; Staff, pp. 107 – 108.

82 Agnes L. Sasscier, "The Quiver of Love," *Hobbies*, February, 1951, pp. 88 – 93.

83 Staff, pp. 105 – 106; Buday, p. 281; Alistair Allen, p. 155.

84 Lee, pp. 71 – 72; Staff, pp. 97 – 98; Buday, p. 282.

85 Staff, pp. 103 – 104.

86 Waterman, p. 247.

87 Marsh, p. 32.

88 Apkarian-Russell, p. 7.

89 Lee, p. 64; Staff, p. 97.

90 McCulloch, p. 169; Fenn and Malpa, p. 209.

91 Buday, p. 278; Allen, p. 149; Lee, pp. 47 – 48.

92 Buday, p. 281; Apkarian-Russell, pp. 19 – 20; Fenn and Malpa, p. 213; Staff, pp. 107 – 108; Allen, p. 154.

93 Apkarian-Russell, p. 18; Staff p. 97; Buday, p. 282; Lee. pp. 72, 75, 82.

94 Chase, p. 71.

95 Staff, p. 112.

96 Staff, p. 112.

97 Marsh, p. 46.

98 Waterman, p. 247.

99 Chase, p. 209.

100 American Greetings: http:/corporate.american greetings.com/aboutus/history.html.

101 Chase, pp. 216 – 217; Buday, p. 264.

102 Chase, p. 206 – 207.

103 Chase, p, 209.

104 Chase, pp. 211 – 212; Buday, p. 279.

105 Chase, pp. 214 – 215.

106 Marsh, p. 32.

107 Marsh, p. 46.

108 Marsh, p. 46.

109 Chase, p. 75.

110 Chase, pp. 75 – 76.

111 Chase, p. 74.

112 Buday, p. 269; Chase, p. 209.

113 Chase, p. 212; Buday, p. 279.

114 Apkarian-Russell, p. 18; Staff, p. 98; Lee, pp. 72 – 75; Buday, p. 282.

115 Waterman, p. 248.

116 Waterman, p. 248.

117 Chase, p. 78.

118 Buday, p. 270; McCulloch, p. 168.

119 Waterman, p. 247.

120 Waterman, p. 246.

121 Marsh, p. 32.

122 Waterman, p. 247.

123 Marsh, p. 52.

124 Chase, p. 67.

125 Waterman, p. 247.

126 Marsh, p. 46.

127 Waterman, p. 246.

128 Marsh, p. 32.

129 Waterman, p. 247; Marsh, p. 40.

130 Waterman, p. 247.

131 Waterman, p. 247.

132 Tariff of 1930: http://uscode.house.gov/download/pls/19C4.txt.

133 Tariff of 1930: http://uscode.house.gov/download/pls/19C4.txt.

134 Staff, p. 112.

135 Marsh, p. 32.

136 Waterman, p. 247.

137 Waterman, p. 247.

138 Waterman, p. 248.

139 Staff, pp. 65 – 66.

140 Staff, pp. 56 – 57, 63, 65 – 70, 87 – 90; Hodgson, p. 148; McCulloch, p. 53; Lee, pp. 76 – 79, 81, 92; Adelaide Hechtlinger and Wilbur Cross, *The Complete Book of Paper Antiques*, New York: Coward, McCann & Geoghegan, Inc., 1972, p; 70.

141 Lee, pp. 81 – 83, 88 – 89, 92, 95; Hechtlinger and Cross, pp. 68 – 70; Staff, pp. 57, 67 – 69, 85; McCullough, p. 53.

142 Lee, pp. 76, 81, 82, 90, 95; Staff, pp. 65, 67, 69, 87; Harper's, pp. 104 – 105.

143 Lee, pp. 84, 86 – 87, 95.

144 Staff, p. 103.

145 Hechtlinger & Cross, p. 68 – 69; Lee, p. 88 – 89.

146 Chase, p. 74.

147 Chase, p. 74.

148 Chase, p. 74.

Bibliography

Allen, Alistair & Joan Hoverstadt, *The History of Printed Scraps*, London: New Cavendish Books, 1983.

Allen, Diane, *The Official Price Guide: Postcards, 1st Edition*, New York: House of Collectibles, 1990.

American Greetings, http:/corporate.americangreetings.com/aboutus/history.html.

Anonymous, "Valentines of the 1880s," *The Grade Teacher*, February 1953, pp. 28-29.

Apkarian-Russell, Pamela E., *Postmarked Yesterday: Art of the Holiday Postcard*, Portland, Oregon: Collector's Press, 2001.

B.M.S. "Our February Cover Story," *Hobbies*, February 1951, p. 95.

Buday, George, *A History of the Christmas Card*, London: Spring Books, 1954.

Campanelli, Dan & Pauline, *Romantic Valentines, A Price Guide*, Gas City, Indiana: L&W Book Sales, 1996.

Chase, Ernest Dudley, *The Romance of Greeting Cards*, Cambridge, Massachusetts: University Press; 1926.

Fenn, Patricia and Alfred P. Malpa, *Rewards of Merit*, The Ephemera Society of America, Charlottesville, Virgina: Howell Press, 1994.

Harper's Weekly, A Journal of Civilization, New York, Saturday, February 13, 1858, Vol. II – No. 59, pp. 104-105.

Hechtlinger, Adelaide and Wilbur Cross, *The Complete Book of Paper Antiques*, New York: Coward, McCann & Geoghegan, Inc., 1972.

Hodgson, Mrs. Willoughby, "Valentines," *The Magazine Antiques*, February; 1930, Vol. XVI, No. 2, pp. 145 – 149.

Holder, Judith, *Sweethearts & Valentines*, New York: A & W Publishers, Inc, 1980.

Karl, Michele, *Greetings with Love, The Book of Valentines*, Gretna, Louisiana: Pelican Publishing Co., Inc., 2003.

Lee, Ruth Webb, *A History of Valentines*, Wellesley Hills, Massachusetts: Lee Publications, The Studio Publications Inc., 5th edition, 1952.

McCulloch, Lou W, *Paper Americana: A Collector's Guide*, San Diego & New York: AS Baines & Co., Inc. also published by London: The Tantivy Press, 1980.

McPherson, Linda, *Collecting Vintage Children's Greeting Cards, Identification and Values*, Paducah, KY: Collector Books, 2006.

Marsh, Jean, *The Illuminated Language of Flowers*, New York: Holt, Rinehart and Winston, 1978.

Nuhn, Roy, "Valentines, Enduring Tokens of Love," *Collector's Showcase*, January/February 1884, Vol. 3, Number 3, pp. 24-29.

Olian, JoAnne, editor, *Children's Fashions 1860 – 1912*, Mineola, New York: Dover Publications, Inc., 1994.

_____ . *Children's Fashions 1900 – 1950*, Mineola, New York: Dover Publications, Inc., 2003.

Sasscier, Agnes L., "The Quiver of Love, " *Hobbies*, February; 1951, pp. 88-93.

Schweitzer, John C., "Transported by Love," *Antiques and Collectibles*, February 1990, pp. 28 – 30.

Smith, Jack H., *Postcard Companion: The Collector's Reference*, Radnor, Pennsylvania: Wallace Homestead Book Company, 1989.

Staff, Frank, *The Valentine & Its Origins*, New York & Washington: Frederick A Praeger Inc. Publishers,1969.

Tariff of 1930: uscode.house.gov/download/pls/19C4.txt.

Waterman, Catherine, *Flora's Lexicon, an Interpretation of the Language and Sentiment of Flowers with an Outline of Botany and a Poetical Introduction*, Boston: Phillips, Sampson, and Company, New York: J.C. Derby, 1857.

Wood, Jane, *The Collector's Guide to Postcards*, Gas City, Indiana: L.W. Promotions, 1984, 1987, 1989.

Index